Getting it Right,

‖‖‖‖‖‖‖‖‖‖‖‖‖‖‖‖‖‖‖‖

D0976612

Getting it Right

Devotionals from the Journal of Candy Pfeifer

By

Candy Pfeifer

©Copyright 2006 by Candy Pfeifer

Published by Royalty I
120 West Court Street
Washington Court House, Ohio 43160

Printed in the United States of America

10 Digit ISBN 1-933858-06-0
13 Digit ISBN 978-1-933858-06-7

Library of Congress Control Number: 2006925315

Acknowledgements

Special thanks to my parents, Don and Thelma Pfeifer, for teaching me about Jesus and setting me on a path of seeking the kingdom of God.

To Jerry Brecheisen, for everything! I wouldn't know where to start.

To my aunt Helen Kritzwiser and my mother, for all those hours of proofreading. (Aunt Helen went to heaven just before this book was published—she *got it right!*)

To my ministry partners—John and Glenda Pfeifer, Mary Jane Carter, Rob Snyder, and Julia Dawson—for sharing my dreams and putting up with me.

To Deana Warren – Thanks for having a heart for our ministry

To all my family members, too numerous to name. I am so blessed to be a part of this family. I love you all!

Foreword

I first met Candy Pfeifer backstage, readying for a concert. I immediately noticed her warm, friendly ease around people, but I also noticed something else. She seemed to possess a quiet confidence in who she was and why she was there. I admired that. I knew it would connect with audiences. I wondered if her confidence was gleaned from lessons learned in the storms, the trenches, and the fire. What seemed completely obvious was her unshakable sense of who she was, as well as *whose* she was.

Within these poignant pages, Candy offers us a peek at the gentle nudges and prodding's which have brought her so far. She offers with gentle grace and candor her personal journey, and the processes she incorporated to make sense of it all. She shares her story at face value, with honesty and vulnerability.

It will bless you. She will bless you. Sharing her pilgrimage will challenge us; understanding it will help us to better understand our own.

JANET PASCHAL

Introduction

Life on the road has had it share of awesome moments as well as personally challenging times. The following pages are taken from my personal journal over a ten-year period in my life, during which I experienced some extremely painful and emotional events. I was prompted to write this book by Mary Jane Carter, one of my ministry partners and dearest friends. I pray that as you read, you will realize that we all struggle with many of the same issues. I pray also that you will rediscover, in a new and refreshing way, that God never fails and that our ability to overcome life-altering events depends on how much we trust Him.

The thing I struggled with most in my life was a spirit of fear. Many of the struggles reflected in my journal entries resulted from submitting to the spirit of fear instead of the Word of God. I believe fear entered me when I was three years old and had to have a minor medical procedure. The procedure required a night in the hospital, and back then parents were not allowed to stay with their children overnight. My mother was asked to leave when visiting hours were over.

I remember sobbing and crying for my mother not to leave. Just recently she told me that she could hear me all the way down the hall, and that leaving me there was the hardest thing she had ever done. Even now, recalling that event makes me teary-eyed for my mother. When Mom left the hospital, I continued to cry for her. A nurse came into the room and told me that if I didn't "shut up" she would put a net over my bed. I had never even heard the word *shut up*, and had certainly never experienced the tone of voice in which it was said. I cowered in the corner of the bed, and I fully believe a spirit of fear entered my mind and my emotions at that time.

As a little girl, I was deathly afraid of the dark and was also afraid of being kidnapped or getting separated from my mother. When my youngest brother came along, I was often afraid that he would get lost. During my teenage years I was afraid of not being accepted, so I did a lot of things I should not have done. In my twenties and thirties, I had fear about my finances, about my health, about my parents' health, and about making a commitment to marry—but I had an even greater fear of being alone the rest of my life.

I was a Christian and was even active in ministry, but I was living in defeat that I didn't understand. One day my brother John called me to the back of the bus and said he felt like the Lord had revealed to him that I had a spirit of fear. You cannot fight an enemy you don't know about, and I didn't have any idea what my problem was until the day God revealed it through John. I received what he said and immediately started seeking God for deliverance.

We were singing in a camp meeting in Florida when I realized that I was at the point of desperation for deliverance from fear. I went to the altar, and as soon as I knelt I knew I had audience with the Almighty God. I was so humbled to be in His presence that I felt as if I couldn't bow low enough. We were meeting in a tent, so I ended up with my face in the sand

and grass. I was weeping freely, with emotion coming from some deep place in my soul. I believe Jesus was gently leading me from the point of being a three-year-old child to my present-day maturity. At the moment my desperation met my faith, and I received my deliverance from fear.

The Bible says in 2 Timothy 1:7, "For God has not given us a spirit of fear, but of power and of love and of a sound mind." Jesus accomplished that on the cross two thousand years ago, yet it took me over forty years to receive the deliverance that had been available to me all along. That curse was broken in my life and the blinders removed. When fear tries to attack me now, I recognize the enemy and know how to fight. Submitting to and believing the Word of God is my spiritual strategy.

Each entry in this book bears both the stain of tears and the blossoms of hope that come with following Jesus. In other words, these are *real* life experiences. Whether you're a full-time singer in a southern gospel group or work in a secular environment, whether you're a Christian leader or a staff member, whether you're married or single, whether you've been walking with the Lord for many years or you're just beginning the Christian life, you will discover the common threads of victory woven into these pages.

Be blessed, be strengthened, and be encouraged. And always remember that God is the heavenly Tailor whose loving skill can turn a heavy coat of fear or failure into a joyous garment of praise.

You are not alone!

CANDY

From My Journal

March 21, 1992

We're somewhere between Duncanville, Pennsylvania, and Atlantic City, New Jersey. The concert in Pennsylvania went great! Hearts were blessed, and lives were changed. I was tired last night, but I awakened feeling good. I took a shower, made coffee, had my devotions, and gave Mom and Dad a call. I was all set to have a perfect day. But as I got into my routine, I could feel that spirit of heaviness creeping over me. I'm still struggling with depression. I know I can get victory over these emotional ups and downs through my relationship with Jesus Christ. There *is* an answer.

What Father Says

"For that He himself has suffered being tempted, He is able to aid those who are tempted" (Hebrews 2:18).

For You Today

The Lord was teaching me that I can't trust my feelings. I awakened feeling good, but before the day was over, I was struggling. Although your feelings can keep you in turmoil, they can't be totally ignored. You're not a robot—you're a human being. Learn to enjoy your good feelings; be thankful for them. And then stay thankful, even when you're not feeling as good. Praise the Lord for the struggle, and ask Him what you can learn through it. The Bible says to give thanks in all things (1 Thessalonians 5:18). That's difficult! But by praising the Lord in spite of your feelings, you steal the devil's ammunition and take authority over him. As a result, he can't ruin your day. Remember, spiritual authority can only be taken through the blood of Jesus Christ.

From My Journal

March 25, 1992

I'm grateful to have time alone with the Lord. During my devotions this morning, I read a Bible verse that really encouraged me. It was a perfect verse for me—and I found it at just the right time! Even though I get a bit discouraged, I know I am growing in the Lord.

What Father Says

"Being confident of this very thing, that He who has begun a good work in you will complete it until the day of Jesus Christ" (Philippians 1:6).

For You Today

There have been times when I have had to claim Philippians 1:6 minute by minute! I am growing; and as I look back, I see that I have grown the most through hard times. I guess the idea of "growing pains" applies in most areas of life. But no matter what happens in your life today, be confident that it is for a purpose. God is at work in you, and He's not finished yet.

Traveling on the Pfeifers' bus, we often enter a construction zone. Sometimes the pavement is all torn up, and there are "Men at Work" signs along the highway. The construction zones slow us down, but we know that the work being done will make it easier for us to travel that road in the future. Spiritually, you are in a construction zone. Although your progress is often impeded, you must remember that the end result will be a beautiful highway that will take you where you need to go. So post a "God at Work" sign on your life and you will keep the devil on the run. Someday you will see the end result: a beautiful road that leads to the very throne of Jesus Christ in heaven.

From My Journal

April 11, 1992

I have been in my new house for about ten days. It is taking me some time to get adjusted. I know it is good for me. I need to grow up in so many areas. Jesus is helping me. How do people ever live without the presence of the Holy Spirit in their lives? I want Him to saturate my spirit, soul, and body.

What Father Says

"We should no longer be children, tossed to and fro and carried about with every wind of doctrine, by the trickery of men, in the cunning craftiness of deceitful plotting, but, speaking the truth in love, may grow up in all things into Him who is the head—Christ" (Ephesians 4:14–15).

For You Today

I grew up in a family of seven. I lived in a dorm at college and then back with my parents before moving into my own home. The responsibility of having my own place made for a rude awakening, but it was exciting at the same time. If you are at a point in life where your responsibilities are weighing you down, realize that your actions and reactions reflect your spiritual maturity level. It may be time to grow. Like weight training, the weight of your burden is increasing your stamina—increasing your spiritual muscle. The Bible says we should "grow up in all things unto Him who is the head—Christ." Don't forget who's in control. Turn your responsibilities over to Christ, and *grow!*

From My Journal

June 4, 1992

I am sitting at my kitchen table, looking out the front window at a sidewalk my roommate, Deb, and I just built. We built it with white rocks and step stones. It's beautiful! My arms are really sore, but it feels good to accomplish something that monumental. With the Lord's help, I am trying to keep my emotions steady. I thank Him every day for healing me physically and emotionally.

My fiancé, Rob, a drummer for the Pfeifers, and I are going out tonight. I'm really looking forward to it. Rob sent me a dozen roses last week—that's a wonderful feeling! I just read my devotions for the day. They were about being an encouraging Christian instead of a judgmental one. *Please, Jesus, help me to do that!*

What Father Says

"So then each of us shall give account of himself to God. Therefore let us not judge one another anymore, but rather resolve this, not to put a stumbling block or a cause to fall in our brother's way" (Romans 4:12–13).

"Therefore comfort each other and edify one another, just as you also are doing" (1 Thessalonians 5: 11).

"Therefore let us pursue the things which make for peace and the things by which one may edify another" (Romans 14:19).

For You Today

The roses were like silent words of encouragement to me. Edifying one another (or encouraging one another) is one of the godliest things you can do. Look around you: self-esteem is at an all-time low. Words of encouragement are the catalyst for healing. Only God knows how powerful they are. Words can be used for either encouragement or judgment. If you want to walk in and receive the blessings of God and His Word, you'll have to do what the Bible says—and it says to edify and encourage, not judge.

It's pretty simple. When you find yourself talking about people in a judgmental way, (which we all have done) think of the Nike commercial slogan and add the word *don't*— "Just *Don't* Do It!" Encouraging people can be a bit intimidating or embarrassing, but do it anyway. The devil hates it when we get in line with the Word. Ask the Lord for holy boldness. At that point, you are being obedient. It is God's will for you to encourage others, and He loves obedience. What better way both to make someone's day and to make your Heavenly Father proud—Just do it!

From My Journal

June 7, 1992

We sang all day yesterday for a city festival in Kansas. We're still here today. Yesterday we were with the Anchormen, The Freemans, and the Johnny Minnick Family. I feel as if we made new friends with Diane and Chris Freeman. Today we will be singing with The Lesters. The family of Tom Tasker, our guitar and trombone player, has been with us the last two days. They are so proud of Tom and extremely happy to be here. I want to portray a Christlike spirit all day today—to everyone.

What Father Says

"A new commandment I give for you today, that you love one another; as I have loved you, that you also love one another. By this all will know that you are my disciples, if you have love for one another" (John 13: 34–35).

"Take My yoke upon you and learn from Me, for I am gentle and lowly in heart, and you will find rest for your souls" (Matthew 11:29).

For You Today

Love, gentleness, and humility are some of the chief characteristics of Christ, characteristics that we must adopt if we are to be His followers. I have to think about these characteristics constantly, and the one I seem to struggle with the most is gentleness. I was raised with four brothers, so I had to learn to be tough sometimes.

One night we sang at the Steve Hurst School of Music in Nashville, Tennessee. After the concert, Steve wanted to pray with each one of us; and when he came to me, he prayed for God to give me a spirit of gentleness. At that moment I broke and wept like a baby. I had never realized that this was something I lacked. Soon the Holy Spirit was bearing a strong witness within me to Steve's prayer. Through my tears, I started saying, "I need that." At that moment, my spirit was doing the talking. Since that day I've been sensitive to the importance of gentleness. I'm not saying that I'm *always* gentle, but I'm working on it.

Think about your own life in these three areas: love, gentleness, and humility. Do you lack one more than the others? (Maybe you feel that you lack all of them!) Allow the Holy Spirit to search your heart, confess your need to the Father through Jesus Christ, and ask Him to fill you each day with the qualities you lack. Tell Him you want to walk, talk, act, and react like Jesus. If you are truly sincere, you'll find yourself growing in each of these areas.

From My Journal

June 21, 1992

We are on the bus, on our way to Uniontown, Pennsylvania. We have been out for ten days, and we're more than ready to go home! I finished writing a song called "The Blood Was Enough," and I also finished the demo. The Lord really helped me. I hope Homeland Records likes it. My brother John has asked me to work in his apartments. It will be good extra income for me. *Thank you, Jesus!*

Tom Tasker informed us that he would be leaving the Pfeifers. Now I'll have to work harder on my saxophone. Jesus will help me. I know that God is doing a work in our ministry. I want to stay open and flexible, especially when it comes to personnel. This group has to be left in the Lord's hands!

What Father Says

"Be anxious for nothing, but in everything by prayer and supplication, with thanksgiving, let your requests be made known to God; and the peace of God, which surpasses all understanding, will guard your hearts and minds through Christ Jesus" (Philippians 4:6–7).

For You Today

The prerequisites to maintaining peace are these: don't worry, be thankful, and tell God through Jesus Christ what you need. The Bible says, "Faith without works is dead" (James 2:26). Our "work" is to trust God and make our needs known to Him. Then our faith kicks in—faith in the fact that God is in control of everything: ministries, finances, health, relationships, job, home, transportation. It's time for you to take a rest! Rest in God's holiness, wisdom, grace, and power. Don't worry, be thankful, and make your needs known. God will take care of everything else.

From My Journal

July 21, 1992

We are singing at a camp meeting in eastern Kentucky this week. Dad is preaching in the evening services, and local pastors are preaching in the morning services. Dad is doing an excellent job. He's preaching like he did when he was a younger man. He is in the Spirit, and we're receiving the blessing. I felt good about our singing tonight. I didn't think it was too great last night. Sometimes we lose our concentration, but Jesus always helps us.

I really treasure the times we work with Dad. If Jesus tarries, there will come a day when I'll be looking back and longing for these times again. I can't think on things like that very much without feeling a little sadness. I have such a great heritage!

Jesus, I want to be more like Grandma Ware in my laughter, more like my mother in my personality, more like my father in my spiritual discernment, and I want to have my grandfather's peaceful nature and anointing for singing. Use me for your glory, Jesus. I love you!

What Father Says

"And so it was, when they had crossed over, that Elijah said to Elisha, 'Ask! What may I do for you, before I am taken away from you?' Elisha said, 'Please let a double portion of your spirit be upon me'" (2 Kings 2:9).

For You Today

According to Scripture, it is possible to receive someone's *mantle* (spirit or anointing). Elijah was a great prophet of God, and he was miraculously taken up into heaven. Elisha, his successor, prayed for and received a double portion of his mentor Elijah's spirit, which empowered his own prophetic ministry.

You may be seeking God's direction and power for your ministry. Deuteronomy 28:2 says, "And all these blessings shall come upon you and overtake you, because you obey the voice of the LORD your God." Obedience is a great place to start when you are seeking God's direction and power. Do what you can do now. Do what God is asking you to do right where you are. When you are obedient in taking the smaller steps it will be easier to take the larger steps. He not only gives us directions but also gives us His Holy Spirit to help us obey them. What a great deal! Go ahead and ask for a double portion of the Holy Spirit to fall upon you. You won't be disappointed!

From My Journal

July 23, 1992

L ast night was so strange for me. I became extremely emotional and cried over my brother Sam's death in an auto accident. I haven't done that in years. My devotional today was on the death of a family member. For the Christian, that's a time to rejoice. Loneliness remains, but contentment overshadows it. I will go to heaven someday and be with Jesus. And I'll see Sam.

I feel very content when I am at a camp meeting with Christian people who have this same hope. I wish I could capture this emotion every day of my life. It's hard for the devil to mess with you on a holiness camp ground, where Jesus is proclaimed and everything is devoted to and in honor of Him.

What Father Says

"Hear my cry, O God; Attend to my prayer. From the end of the earth I will cry For you today, When my heart is overwhelmed; Lead me to the rock that is higher than I" (Psalm 61:1–2).

"Blessed be the Lord, Who daily loads us with benefits" (Psalm 68:19a).

For You Today

It amazes me how our Heavenly Father gives us exactly what we need, when we need it. The day I needed comfort about the death of a loved one, my devotions were about that very thing. Situations like that happen to me all the time. You and I need to recognize them when they do. The Scriptures say that God "daily loads us with benefits." I didn't realize at the time that I could have the same feeling of strength and security anywhere. Being surrounded with loving Christian brothers and sisters is wonderful, but it isn't our outside circumstances that dictate our happiness. We carry the Holy Spirit of Jesus Christ inside of our spirit. The happiness of Christ's presence is like a well springing up within us.

Our mind, will, and emotions are affected by our circumstances, which is why we have to keep our minds renewed. How do we do that? By reading the word of God, speaking positively, and thinking on things that are pure, lovely and of good report. The Bible also says to pray without ceasing, be in an attitude of prayer, and always be aware of the Father's presence. When you do that, it will give you the feeling of comfort, strength, and security for which we are all searching.

From My Journal

October 21, 1992

We are on the bus headed for Chicago. Kathy's grandmother, Madeline Peyton, died yesterday. Kathy has been my friend since I was nine-years-old, and she helped to found our group. I wish I could have gone to the funeral with her. *Please, Jesus, comfort that family today, and protect Kathy as she travels to Roanoke. Thank-you!* Yesterday I found out that we will be recording a new project with Larry Goss. That's exciting! We need Jesus to help us find the right songs.

What Father Says

"Yea, though I walk through the valley of the shadow of death, I will fear no evil; for you are with me; your rod and staff, they comfort me" (Psalm 23:4).

For You Today

Although Psalm 23:4 seems to be directed toward the dying, I believe family members and friends also can take comfort in this scripture. Emotionally, we walk through the "valley of the shadow of death" with our loved one. The fear of loneliness and loss can be overwhelming. Yet according to this Psalm, we do not have to fear. God is always there to comfort us.

As I write this, the Father has told me that dying to self is also a valley we have to walk through. Dying to self means putting God and others first. That makes you vulnerable. People may take advantage of that. But the Psalmist says of God, "Your rod and your staff they comfort me." God is with you not only in person but also in *power*. Don't be afraid. God has you covered by His presence, His power, and His wisdom (James 1:5). Dying to self is an ongoing process. Don't be discouraged; just strive to do what the Word says, and trust God to take care of the rest.

From My Journal

January 11, 1995

Almost three years have passed since my roommate Deb was married. Living alone is something I never thought I could do. As I look back, God has been doing a wonderful healing in my life. He worked it out for me to keep my house. *Thank you, Jesus!* I'm also thankful for His help with several Pfeifer projects. Our Homeland recording project was produced by Russell Mauldin and entitled the "The Blood Was Enough." I was so excited! The next project was produced by Otis Forest, and I was signed to Century Music as a writer. I had four cuts on our *Stand Strong* project. We'll be recording again in February and March. I love the studio!

Teresa, our piano player, left us last year, and it has been a real struggle but I believe it is for the best. Teresa is very talented, and I love her like a sister; but she seems happy. We have a new piano player from Alabama named Stan Sheridan. He's a great guy!

Rob has asked me to marry him. I am waiting on an answer from the Lord about marriage. The Lord told me to keep my house, so He will guide me about this decision, as well. The group has been signed to Century II Talent Agency, and as of April 1, 1995, will be booked exclusively through it. We've been booked on *Grand Ole Opry* in May. *Thank you, Jesus!*

What Father Says

"Trust in the LORD with all your heart, And lean not on your own understanding; In all your ways acknowledge Him, And He shall direct your paths" (Proverbs 3:5–6).

For You Today

Loneliness and fear are evil cousins. Maybe you're living on the edge. Maybe some dark clouds are drifting over your life—in your relationships or in your career. I understand. I never thought I would be alone in 1995—or even now, as a matter fact. It was always one of my biggest fears. Yet the Lord delivered me from the spirit of fear, and with His authority I will not allow it to win any battles in my life.

Having that kind of determination will hold you steady in uncertain times. Are you alone and lonely? Do you have a fear of the future? The wisdom writer said, "Trust in the LORD with all your heart." Choose to acknowledge His sovereignty. Believe what He promised in His Word. Let Him be your guide through the winding ways of your life. You may be anxious about the future, but you can rest assured that God knows all about it. In fact He's already been to your future. He knows what road you should take. Don't let the enemy confuse you. Take your thoughts into captivity, and speak His Word to your situation—out loud!

From My Journal

October 7, 1996

After many months of not writing, I am led to begin journaling again. I am in constant turmoil about many things—my parents' health, the fact that they are getting older, my own health, and my wedding date. I don't think I have ever been this confused. I had a wonderful talk with my mother the other day, and she told me that I have a tendency to overreact. I agree!

Today I read in Proverbs 17:22 that "a cheerful heart is good medicine, but a crushed spirit dries up the bones." Happiness is a matter of how we act and react to life situations. I need to be more cheerful and positive. I need to acknowledge that God will take care of my parents, that He will watch over my health, and that He will give me wisdom about my wedding. What comfort! It makes my soul cheerful. *Thank you, Father!*

What Father Says

"The spirit of a man will sustain him in sickness, but who can bear a broken spirit?" (Proverbs 18:14).

For You Today

onfusion is one of the devil's schemes. It has no place in the Christian's life. I have discovered that when confusion tries to come against me, I must get into the Word, pray for direction, get my spiritual armor in place, and believe like a child. Every day includes a series of choices. What to wear. What to eat. Where to go. What to do. Be careful not to be caught in the web of indecision. It is a trap that may break your spirit. Trust God. Listen for His stops and His starts.

As a Christian, your armor includes salvation, righteousness, faith, truth, and peace. And your weapon is the Word of God. God doesn't want you to wander in the desert of confusion. He wants you to live by the cool streams of His care.

From My Journal

October 8, 1996

We are on the bus headed for a television taping in Pittsburgh, Pennsylvania. The trees are starting to change, and the air is crisp. What a beautiful day. *God, you are so good to us!* I read in Colossians that as one of God's chosen people, I am to be compassionate and forgiving. Most of all, I am to reflect God's holiness with a loving heart. I must let the Holy Spirit work through me so that these characteristics will be displayed in my life. I am so blessed and so happy to serve the Maker of goodness!

What Father Says

"Love suffers long and is kind; love does not envy; love does not parade itself, is not puffed up; does not behave rudely, does not seek its own, is not provoked, thinks no evil; does not rejoice in iniquity, but rejoices in the truth; bears all things, believes all things hopes all things, endures all things. Love never fails" (1 Corinthians 13:4–8a).

For You Today

God's timing never ceases to amaze me. Within the last few days, He has been dealing with me on the subject of love. I've often heard it said that love can't be explained, but it can. The Bible defines it perfectly in 1 Corinthians 13. The commentary in my Bible includes such explanations as this: "Love suffers long, having patience with imperfect people. Love is kind and active in doing good. Love does not envy; it actually wants other people to get ahead."

I'm learning that love not only includes our affections; it also includes our actions and our attention. When you are patient you are expressing Christ's love. When you are helping someone you are sharing His love. When you want the best for another, you are reflecting the love of Jesus. Love is an outward expression of your inward relation to God through His Son. It is a natural reaction to God's acceptance.

From My Journal

October 12, 1996

M y devotions this morning were about not being able to earn salvation. It was timely for me. Even when I'm confused and fighting negative feelings, my spiritual life can stay strong by believing in the power of Jesus blood. I do believe in that power. I am protected by it, and the devil can't do a thing about that! We are in Illinois, singing outdoors with two other groups I had not heard before. It's another beautiful day, and being outside feels nice. I feel good today. I am so thankful for my life and for what the Lord allows me to do through music. *I love you, Jesus!*

What Father Says

"He has delivered us from the power of darkness and conveyed us into the kingdom of the Son of His love" (Colossians 1:13).

For You Today

The key word in today's scripture is the word *has*. God *has* already delivered us from the power of darkness—that was accomplished two thousand years ago at Calvary! These promises and provisions are yours to claim. For you, darkness may represent depression or every hopeless feeling you have. If you truly believe what the Word says, you must rest on the promise that you *already* have been delivered from darkness. Satan will still come against you; but as you remain in the Word, you can use it as a weapon against him. First John 4:4 says, "You are of God, little children, and have overcome them, because He who is in you is greater than he who is in the world." In other words, your heavenly Father can whup anyone on the block!

From My Journal

October 14, 1996

I'm thankful for the roses in my life, although I don't deny that there are thorns. My roses are the love of my family and friends, music, food, shelter, transportation, and most of all, Jesus! As for the thorns, I give them over to God my Father. They can't stick to Him! Some of my thorns are "homemade." When I refuse to live by God's Word, I'm the one who suffers. I must rid myself of those attitudes or actions that don't honor Christ and show respect for others. I have taken off my old self and put on my new self.

I am one of God's chosen. I am holy, and He dearly loves me. Therefore I will be compassionate, kind, humble, gentle, and patient. I will be forgiving as God forgave me. Most important, I will love. Christ's love through me binds all of these qualities together in perfect unity.

What Father Says

"But now you yourselves are to put off all these: anger, wrath, malice, blasphemy, filthy language out of your mouth. Do not lie to one another, since you have put off the old man with his deeds, and have put on the new man who is renewed in knowledge according to the image of Him who created him. . . . Therefore, as the elect of God, holy and beloved, put on tender mercies, kindness, humility, meekness, longsuffering; bearing with one another, and forgiving one another, if anyone has a complaint against another; even as Christ forgave you, so you also must do. But above all these things put on love, which is the bond of perfection" (Colossians 3:8–10).

For You Today

Almost everything we deal with in life, good or bad, is linked to our relationships. These scriptures give us a manual for strengthening relationships and becoming obedient children of God. The result: "The peace of God will rule our hearts" (Colossians 3:15).

There are some things that you will have to "put off." Get rid of your anger. It not only hurts others; it hurts you in the process. Get rid of deceit. Live an open and honest life. Avoid altering the "facts" to increase your status. Like removing a heavy coat, put off the things that are not like Christ.

There are also things that you will put on. Clothe yourself with kindness, forgiveness, and patience. Let the character of Christ be evident in you. The result: peace.

Peace is what I am striving for. How about you?

From My Journal

October 24, 1996

Myy devotions today were on love. I have such a long way to go to love consistently. I talk too much, and I'm too opinionated. I want to get to the place where I give my opinion only when asked. The book of Proverbs if filled with truth . . . if only I could make a lifestyle out of it. Even when I feel like I'm obtaining these biblical qualities, it's tempting to let pride in. It's hard for me to define my role as a godly woman, the role with which my Father is most pleased. I'll keep working on it.

What Father Says

"And let us not grow weary while doing good, for in due season we shall reap if we do not lose heart" (Galatians 6:9).

"For whom the Lord loves He chastens, and scourges every son whom He receives. If you endure chastening, God deals with you as with sons; for what son is there whom the father does not chasten?" (Hebrews 12: 6–7).

For You Today

God is constantly at work in my life, improving my character qualities as I respond in obedience to His Word. There are times when I have felt His gentle correction, and times when I've been discouraged by my lack of progress. But I know He will not give up on me, and He won't give up on *you*. You are His child. He loves you even when He is correcting you. He delights in you. He wants what is best for you. He speaks encouragement and instruction by His Holy Spirit and through His holy Word. Keep striving to line up with Scripture, and as time goes on you will reap the benefit of a godly lifestyle. Ask the Lord to help you hear and sense His correction, and then react positively to it.

From My Journal

October 25, 1996

Today I feel like if I don't talk to my fiancé Rob, I'll burst! I have so much spinning in my head about the future. I'm having such doubts about marriage. I even have doubts about myself. God my Father knows, and He is totally in control. I need to chill!

What Father Says

"It shall come to pass that before they call, I will answer; And while they are still speaking, I will hear" (Isaiah 65:24).

"You will keep him in perfect peace, whose mind is stayed on You, because he trusts in You" (Isaiah 26:3).

For You Today

God proves Himself in every situation, yet we still worry. It makes me feel bad that God is so ignored! As human beings, we're frustrated when we know we're right about something and people won't believe us. Can you imagine how God feels? He is perfect in every way, yet His own people often refuse to believe His truths.

Peace of mind is a choice. You either chose to trust God or the devil. That sounds dramatic, but it's true. If you are constantly worrying, you are not fully trusting. If Satan can keep you in a worried, stressed-out state of mind, he wins. (Don't you hate it when that happens?) When you trust in God, you win.

Are you worried? Focus on God instead of focusing on problems. Learn to live in "perfect peace." Believe in God the way you want people to believe in you! Think of it—even before you ask God's answer is on the way.

From My Journal

October 30, 1996

It's 7:30 a.m. We're in Florida, and it's the start of a beautiful day. We are preparing to sing at a breakfast club. *Thank you for life, Father!* I just read a devotional from *Our Daily Bread* that asked this question: "Do others sense the fragrance of Christ when they are with you?" More than anything, I want to be a Christlike woman!

What Father Says

"Nevertheless the solid foundation of God stands, having this seal: 'The Lord knows those who are His,' and, 'Let everyone who names the name of Christ depart from iniquity.' But in a great house there are not only vessels of gold and silver, but also of wood and clay, some for honor and some for dishonor. Therefore if anyone cleanses himself from the latter, he will be a vessel for honor, sanctified and useful for the Master, prepared for every good work" (2 Timothy 2:19–21).

For You Today

B eing Christlike starts with being obedient to His Word, and sensitive to the gentle whispers of the Holy Spirit. Second Timothy 2:19–21 is clear about how a Christian should act. When you mess up—as we all do—choose not to walk in discouragement or an attitude that says, "I can't live up to this!" Rather, repent and move on. God knows that we start our spiritual journey as a vessel of clay. But His Word declares that we don't have to stay that way. Seek to be a vessel of honor. Stay in the Word, keep praying, keep serving, and keep saying "Yes!" to God. I guarantee that others will soon "sense the fragrance of Christ" in you!

From My Journal

November 5, 1996

I am listening to Senator Robert Dole's concession speech. I'm upset that he didn't win the White House, and I'm sad to say that this is the first presidential election in which I have voted. Middle-class Christian Americans often refuse to stand up for what they believe. God is not pleased! *Forgive me, Father, for being so apathetic.*

I feel that I need to be more disciplined with my devotions and my diet. My soul needs to be fed more, but not my body! I will do something about it—I really want to be a blessed woman.

What Father Says

"Praise the Lord. Blessed is the man who fears the Lord, who finds great delight in His commands. His children will be mighty in the land; each generation of the upright will be blessed. Wealth and riches are in His house, and His righteousness endures forever. Even in darkness light dawns for the upright, for the gracious and compassionate and righteous man. Good will come to him who is generous and lends freely, who conducts his affairs with justice. Surely he will never be shaken; a righteous man will be remembered forever. He will have no fear of bad news; his heart is secure, he will have no fear; in the end he will look in triumph on his foes. He has scattered abroad his gifts to the poor, his righteousness endures forever; his horn will be lifted high in honor" (Psalm 112:1–9).

For You Today

Fulfilling my responsibility to vote for our nation's leaders is just one of the things God revealed to me that was lacking in my life. If I am to "delight in His commands," which includes showing respect for all who are in authority (Rom. 13:1), I will not only practice my citizenship by voting but will also *pray* for those in authority (1 Tim. 2:2). Why in the world wouldn't we get out and help to elect godly people to be in authority over us?

I think the devil has totally deceived Christian America in this area. It's called the spirit of apathy. It's a very subtle plan to take down our nation while we allow immoral, godless politicians to be elected. Thank God the Christian community elected a born again president in the 2000 election, even if it was by a very small margin. In my opinion, it should have been a landslide!

According to Psalm 112, part of the blessing is triumphing over our foes. And one of our greatest foes is the spirit of apathy. A righteous person does what is right. And voting is the right thing to do. Don't forget to pray that our leaders will be led by the Holy Spirit. Revival in Washington would be an incredible thing! But revival in Washington begins with revival in your own heart.

From My Journal

November 7, 1996

I am reading a lot about resting in the Lord. I need that right now, more than anything. Last night I awakened in the middle of the night with a prayer on my lips about being secure in the Lord. This morning my devotions have been about that very thing. I know that is not just happenstance. Jesus said in Mathew 11:28–30, "Come to me all you who are weary and burdened, and I will give you rest. Take my yoke upon you and learn from me, for I am gentle and humble in heart, and you will find rest for your souls. For my yoke is easy and my burden is light."

What Father Says

"Those who hope in the Lord will renew their strength. They will soar on wings like eagles; they will run and not grow weary, they will walk and not faint" (Isaiah 40:31).

For You Today

There are so many times in my life when I need rest—not only for my physical body but also for my soul. Life can take its toll if we let it. Inner turmoil can be both physically and spiritually exhausting. It's in those times that we are invited to come to Jesus. He promised to give us much-needed rest. Part of my anxiety at that point in my life was a medical problem experienced by my mother. I am learning to trust the Lord for my parents' health. (I might as well; He is in control anyway!) Anxiety will sap our strength. But if we believe the Word and put our hope in the Lord, our strength will be renewed, we will soar on wings like eagles, run and not grow weary, walk and not faint! *Praise you, Father!*

From My Journal

November 8, 1996

My Grandma Pfeifer left the care facility today. She went home for good—she is in heaven, with a new, eternally strong and healthy body. I imagine she was met by Grandpa Pfeifer, Grandma and Grandpa Cartright, and my brother Sam. I know they were so glad to see her. *I'm glad she's finally home. Father. I know You'll take good care of her. Tell her we'll all be there soon!*

With all the new things the Holy Spirit is revealing to me as I grow, I want to enjoy the new without forgetting the old. Jesus said in Mathew 13:52, "Bring out of your storeroom new treasures as well as old."

What Father Says

"In the same way, younger people should be willing to be under older people. And all of you should be very humble with each other. 'God is against the proud, but He gives grace to the humble'" (1 Peter 5:5).

For You Today

I have been blessed with a godly heritage. All of my grandparents are with Jesus today; and the word *grand* truly describes them. I have learned so much from each one of them. Since my Grandma Pfeifer was mentioned, I'll tell you a story about her. In her later years, Grandma was diagnosed with Alzheimer's disease. She stayed with Mom and Dad as long as they could keep her, but when her condition deteriorated they had to put her in a nursing home.

Naturally, Grandma was unable to tend to her own finances, so Mom and Dad took care of her money and paid her bills. When she was still able, Grandma would go to church with them every Sunday. Grandma had always been a big giver, so each Sunday as the treasurers counted the offering they found tissues in with the money. They knew Anna Pfeifer had given all she had available. Even when she could no longer speak coherently, Grandma would stand up, wave her handkerchief, and praise the Lord—and the glory would fall on the service. It was amazing how her offering of tissues and praise affected an entire congregation!

Giving and praising are only two of many things I have learned from little Anna Pfeifer. May God help you to understand the value of godly senior citizens. Be willing to submit yourself to them, and truly honor them while they are still here.

From My Journal

November 10, 1996

I had to get up at 5:00 a.m. today—ugh! We are headed for a service in Circleville, Ohio. As I was praying in the back of the bus, the sun started to peek through the clouds. It had been snowing all through the night. I felt such oneness with my heavenly Father. How I wish I could maintain that security through all the hours of the day. I can. It's up to me. I lit the candles on the bus this morning. It's cold outside but very warm in here. This is a good place to be. God is so good!

What Father Says

"For you created my inmost being; you knit me together in my mothers womb. I praise you because I am fearfully and wonderfully made; your works are wonderful, I know that full well" (Psalm 139:13–14).

"Are not two sparrows sold for a penny? Yet not one of them will fall to the ground apart from the will of the Father. And even the very hairs of your head are numbered. So don't be afraid; you are worth more than many sparrows" (Matthew 10:29–31).

For You Today

Security. Isn't that what we all desire? There are times when I feel very secure and times when I feel very insecure. When I feel insecure, I'm not trusting the Word; I'm trusting my feelings. That's wrong! If the Creator of the universe takes time to count the hairs on my head, He must be pretty interested in me! He's interested in you as well. Security can be instilled in a child by its earthly parents. In most cases—and there are exceptions—secure people have had secure parents who were able to instill that value in their children. If a child can gather security from earthly parents who have imperfections, how much more can you and I be secure in Jesus Christ, who is perfect! Believe the Word and know who you are in Jesus. He knows everything about you—right down to the number of hairs on your head. And He still loves you, is proud of you, and thinks you are wonderful. Trust Him!

From My Journal

November 14, 1996

I fasted Tuesday and Wednesday. Wow! I have never experienced that before. God was so near that it seemed like I had His full attention. It was a blessed time, and I feel like I found some answers. Now I need to bind fear and rest in the Lord! During my fast I felt as if the Lord gave me Psalm 126. Today the Lord gave me Psalm 34 through my *Our Daily Bread* devotional.

What Father Says

"While they were worshiping the Lord and fasting, the Holy Spirit said, 'Set apart for me Barnabas and Saul for the work to which I have called them.' So after they had fasted and prayed, they placed their hands on them and sent them off" (Acts 13:2).

"Paul and Barnabas appointed elders for them in each church and, with prayer and fasting, committed them to the Lord in whom they had put their trust" (Acts 14:23).

For You Today

Paul and Barnabas prayed, fasted, committed themselves to God, and trusted Him. For some reason when we pray and fast, trust seems to follow naturally. Trusting the Lord is where spiritual battles are won. The Word talks about being made strong in our weakness. When we fast we become weak in body but strong in spirit. As our spirits become stronger, we can hear what the Holy Spirit is saying. I am sorry to say that this occasion in 1996 was the first time I had fasted. One reason it's difficult to fast is that it is so effective; that makes the devil fight extremely hard in this area.

In Mark 9 we read of a time when Jesus' disciples were unable to drive a demon out of a deaf and dumb boy. When they asked why they lacked the power to do it, Jesus said, "It only comes by prayer and fasting." If there is that much spiritual power in fasting, don't think for a minute the devil won't fight you when you fast and pray. But the Holy Spirit will empower you to do it. Remember, greater is He that is in you than he that is in the world!

From My Journal

November 20, 1996

I played a recording session yesterday in Wheelersburg, Ohio. It was for Ed Carter's group. The other players were Dale Scraggs and Joel (from Karen Peck's group), and a piano player and steel picker that I had never met. Gregg Tingler was the producer. It was a very nice day and I felt like everything turned out well. We worked from noon Tuesday to 5:30 a.m. Wednesday. My fingers have blisters on their blisters! I hope this experience will open some doors for me in the studio. It's in God's hands!

What Father Says

"'For my thoughts are not your thoughts, neither are your ways my ways,' declares the Lord. 'As the heavens are higher than the earth, so are my ways higher than your ways and my thoughts than your thoughts'" (Isaiah 55:8–9).

"Commit to the Lord whatever you do, and your plans will succeed" (Proverbs 16:3).

For You Today

At that time, the Lord didn't see fit to give me steady studio work. I had only a few calls, but felt as if I could do a good job if given the chance. Now it seems that we may have a studio of our own—we'll see what happens. I try to walk through doors that I think are opening; but if I'm wrong, I don't get disappointed. According to the Scripture, if I commit whatever I do to the Lord, my plans will succeed. God's ways are definitely higher than ours. Rest in Him for the journey. He knows where you're going. You may think you deserve a "break." You may, and I would love that for you, but God is in control of the "breaks." His way is perfect and His timing is perfect.

From My Journal

November 26, 1996

It's a snowy, windy day today, but I have a warm house to live in. God is so good! In preparation for our wedding I am going through a marriage counseling book and answering questions. It's good for all relationships, and practically teaches the sanctified life. Rob is struggling with getting married now, but he will be fine because he is a spiritual man. It's comforting to know that his steps are ordered by God.

What Father Says

"I am coming to you now, but I say these things while I am still in the world, so that they may have the full measure of my joy within them. I have given them your word and the world has hated them, for they are not of the world any more than I am of the world. My prayer is not that you take them out of the world but that you protect them from the evil one. They are not of the world, even as I am not of it. Sanctify them by the truth; your word is truth. As you sent me into the world, I have sent them into the world. For them I sanctify myself, that they too may be truly sanctified" (John 17:13–19).

For You Today

S anctified means to be set apart for holy use. It's encouraging to know that Jesus prayed this prayer for us—and His prayers are eternal. This prayer is as effective today as when He prayed it. He set Himself apart to do the will of the Father: giving His life to pay the penalty for our sin. His death also provided us with spiritual power to live a sanctified life.

Living a sanctified life simply means living a life set apart. Set apart *from* what? From the devil and his purposes. Set apart *for* what? To do God's will and to help in the building of His kingdom. How do we do that? We make a complete surrender of ourselves to God—giving every-thing we know about ourselves to everything we know about Him (Romans 12:1–2). The result is that we love God completely and love people unconditionally. God helps us to put others first and to live unselfishly. That's where the full measure of Christ's joy comes in. *Jesus, help us to know the truth. And help us to practice it in our daily lives.*

From My Journal

December 2, 1996

Many things were said last weekend that shouldn't have been said. Rob and I are having some pretty intense discussions. *Please, Father, give me a calm, loving spirit, and a closed mouth. Help me to speak only when it makes things better. I need Your wisdom now more than ever!*

What Father Says

"If anyone among you thinks he is religious, and does not bridle his tongue but deceives his own heart, this one's religion is useless" (James 1:26).

"The quiet words of the wise are more to be heeded than the shouts of a ruler of fools" (Ecclesiastes 9:17).

For You Today

How powerful our words are! The Bible says in James 3 that the tongue is a restless evil, full of deadly poison. Wow! It also says no one can tame the tongue. Fortunately, we have the power of the Holy Spirit to help us tame the tongue; there is no way to do it on our own. As I look back on that weekend, I realize that many things were said out of anger and frustration; therefore, nothing was received. Once again I see the Bible being proven: we absolutely cannot operate outside of its wisdom.

When issues are confronted with love and soft answers, they are usually resolved. The reason most of us want to confront when we are angry or frustrated is because we feel bold at those times; we are being driven by anger or frustration. Confrontation is good if it is God-led. But timing is important. Pray for wisdom in such situations. Don't let your mind get clouded with emotions. Say everything out of love. That's what Jesus did!

From My Journal

December 6, 1996

My mother was diagnosed with Parkinson's disease yesterday. It is so hard to understand. She is in good spirits; her attitude is always good. I would like to be one-third the woman she is. My mother kept her life clean, so she doesn't have a bunch of garbage to deal with. I throw the garbage out, and then the devil carries it back in. I think it's time to burn it all through the power of Jesus Christ and through His blood! *Jesus, I really want you to heal my mom!*

What Father Says

"Do not let your hearts be troubled. Trust in God; trust also in me" (John 14:1).

"When evening came, many who were demon-possessed were brought to Him, and He drove out the spirits with a word and healed all the sick" (Matthew 8:16).

"And my God will meet *all* your needs according to His glorious riches in Christ Jesus" (Philippians 4:19 *emphasis mine*).

For You Today

From the day of Mother's diagnosis, I have lived in hope of her manifested healing. I do believe it is God's will to heal us. Just as I live in hope of heaven and Christ's return, I will live with the hope of healing. The Word is all about hope, and I refuse to live without it.

The subject of healing as been very controversial, and I know God is not pleased with that. Believe what you believe, but don't be argumentative. It is a time when Christians must be unified. We must face the enemy with united strength. There are things we all share. One is the sovereignty of God. He has the last word in everything. I learn these things from Scripture: (1) I must trust in God, (2) I must live in expectation, and (3) I must believe that He will meet all our needs.

From My Journal

December 13, 1996

It's a dreary day. The bright spot is that my friend Kathy had her baby on December 11, and I was there. The baby's name is Hannah Noel. I think that is so pretty! Other things in my life aren't as pretty right now. I'm feeling angry toward another person. I don't like to write about negative feelings, so I won't write much today. Life is hard—but God is good.

What Father Says

"The thief comes only to steal and kill and destroy; I have come that they may have life, and have it to the full" (John 10:10).

"Take my yoke upon you and learn from me, for I am gentle and humble in heart, and you will find rest for your souls. For my yoke is easy and my burden is light" (Matthew 11:29–30).

For You Today

I f we believe the Word completely, we know that although life is some-times difficult, Jesus came to give us His joy—life to "the full." That sounds pretty good to me. Jesus said, "My yoke is easy and my burden is light." The burden is light because we are yoked to Jesus. The way I was feeling the day I wrote this journal entry was just the opposite of what Jesus said. I had to decide whether to believe my feelings or believe Him. I was angry at a particular individual that day. Instead of being angry, I should have been prayerful and compassionate. Jesus said He was "gentle and humble," and I should learn from Him.

At this point in my life, I try never to entertain negative thoughts. It isn't easy, but it's possible as we focus on what Jesus said in His Word. Our enemy, Satan, wants you and me to see the dark side of everything. Be willing to pray, to be compassionate, and to do whatever the Lord tells you to do. In the midst of troubling questions, God will show us a miracle—like Hannah Noel.

From My Journal

December 28, 1996

Our sound man, Rob Snyder, married Kris today. It was a beautiful wedding. I am still struggling with my own marriage plans and God is still good!

What Father Says

"Though I walk in the midst of trouble, you preserve my life; you stretch out your hand against the anger of my foes, with your right hand you save me." (Psalm 138:7).

"Do not cast away your confidence, which has great reward. For you have need of endurance, so that after you have done the will of God, you may receive the promise" (Hebrews 10: 35–36).

For You Today

The anger I feel towards my foes comes from the devil himself. The Bible says we do not fight against flesh and blood but against principalities and powers; that is, we fight against Satan and his demonic armies. James the apostle gives us light on the source of our struggles. First, we know that God doesn't add them to our plate. James 1:13 says, "Let no one say when he is tempted, 'I am tempted by God'; for God cannot be tempted by evil, nor does He Himself tempt anyone." Second, God is the source of deliverance. James 1:17 says, "Every good gift and every perfect gift is from above, and comes down from the Father of lights, with whom there is no variation or shadow of turning."

So if God isn't the source of our struggles, we know that Satan must be. As Jesus said, "The thief does not come except to steal, and to kill, and to destroy" (John 10:10). Whether you are struggling with health problems, finances, relationship troubles, or anything else, you can know that it is Satan and not God who placed them in your life.

It is true that much of what we deal with results from of our own poor choices. And sometimes God *allows* the devil to take us through struggles so that we will learn (remember Job?). God can even use the devil for a good purpose. Satan hates that!

From My Journal

January 5, 1997

Rob and I were supposed to get married February 14, but we decided not to. I don't know what will happen now. I'm living day to day and trying my best to trust the Lord. When I truly trust in Him, I feel really peaceful. How I wish I could do that constantly! I am so inconsistent. One thing I know is that I love Jesus, His sacrifice, and His patience with me. I believe in God the Father, God the Son, and His Holy Spirit that He sent to live within me and to comfort me! I want to commit Psalm 34 to memory. Here is a portion of this great Psalm . . .

What Father Says

I will bless the LORD at all times;
His praise shall continually be in my mouth.
My soul shall make its boast in the LORD;
The humble shall hear of it and be glad.
Oh, magnify the LORD with me,

And let us exalt His name together.

I sought the LORD, and He heard me,

And delivered me from all my fears.

They looked to Him and were radiant,

And their faces were not ashamed.

This poor man cried out, and the LORD heard him

And saved him out of all his troubles.

The angel of the LORD encamps all around those who fear Him

And delivers them.

Oh, taste and see that the LORD is good;

Blessed is the man who trusts in Him!

For You Today

K nowing and believing the basic truth of who you are in Jesus—and who He is to you—will comfort you through confusing times. Rob and I went around that same mountain of whether or not to get married three times, living in confusion, but not wanting to let go. Sometimes I still have to let go day by day. I know God is up to something, I just wish He would hurry. In the meantime, I'll keep reading Psalm 34.

If you are at a time in your life that doesn't make much sense, know that through faith in the Lord Jesus Christ, you are still saved—you are still a child of God. He loves you. He is working everything for your good, and has everything under control.

Relax!

From My Journal

January 6, 1997

I read Psalm 34 again today and I feel good. I have had a special time with the Lord. I need to get it through my thick head that all my happiness and contentment comes through drawing near to God!

What Father Says

"Do not be anxious about anything, but in everything, by prayer and petition, with thanksgiving, present your requests to God. And the peace of God, which transcends all understanding, will guard your hearts and your minds in Christ Jesus.

"I am not saying this because I am in need, for I have learned to be content whatever the circumstances. I know what it is to be in need, and I know what it is to have plenty. I have learned the secret of being content in any and every situation, whether well fed or hungry, whether living in plenty or in want. I can do everything through Him who gives me strength" (Philippians 4: 6–7, 11–13).

For You Today

I f I read these verses correctly, the happiness and contentment we are all looking for comes through having a thankful attitude—in spite of our circumstances. The Bible tells us that we should enter His gates with thanksgiving, so it's obvious that a thankful heart draws us near to God. Try being thankful for everything, even the bad stuff.

As Christians, anything we go through serves a greater purpose. As I've said, our Father doesn't bring bad things on us, but He can let them happen to teach us something. You don't have to pray, "Lord I'm so thankful I just wrecked my car," or "Praise God! My kids are out of control." But you can pray, "Lord, I thank you for helping me through this time. Help me to learn what you are trying to teach me (and please do it quickly!)."

Stop complaining. Be thankful. It will change your life!

From My Journal

January 12, 1997

What an incredible day in the Lord. I am spiritually fat today. This morning I worshipped at Open Door, the church my brother Mark founded and pastors. I had lunch with my brother John and his wife, Glenda, and Matt. This evening I worshipped at Kingsway Fellowship. Mark preached a tremendous sermon on John the Baptist this morning, and then tonight Rob preached an anointed sermon on the source, the scope, and salvation.

What Father Says

"Finally, be strong in the Lord and in His mighty power. Put on the full armor of God so that you can take your stand against the devil's schemes" (Ephesians 6:10–11).

For You Today

Being strong in the Lord, or "spiritually fat" as I wrote in my journal, has a lot to do with where you choose to worship and which pastor you chose to submit to. I realize that we will stand alone at the judgment and that we are responsible for picking up the fork and feeding ourselves spiritually. I also know that I can't survive on a steady diet of spiritual junk food. I don't want to waste my time in a church where the glory of the Holy Spirit is not manifested. For me, that would be living on "junk food."

You might say, "You are responsible to read the Word for yourself." Yes I am, but the Bible says "how shall they hear without a preacher?" (Romans 10:14). Part of our personal responsibility, along with Bible reading and prayer, is to become part of a church where Jesus is moving and the Word is preached by an anointed pastor.

I'm not talking about perfection—no pastor is perfect. I'm talking about a pastor who knows truth about the Word, himself, and his people. The Lord wants you to be well fed spiritually and to be strong in Him. If you are a God seeker, He will direct you to the place you need to be.

From My Journal

January 19, 1997

L ast night we drove home from a concert in Michigan. We sang with the Gold City Quartet. God honored us, and we found favor with the people. It was fun. *Thank you, Father, for the gift of joy and for granting us the opportunities that make us happy. All good things are from you.* Tonight we will be in Cincinnati at a Church of God.

What Father Says

"David told the leaders of the Levites to appoint their brothers as singers to sing joyful songs, accompanied by musical instruments: lyres, harp and cymbals" (1 Chronicles 15:16).

"Nehemiah said, 'Go and enjoy choice food and sweet drinks, and send some to those who have nothing prepared. This day is sacred to our Lord. Do not grieve, for the joy of the Lord is your strength'" (Nehemiah 8:10).

For You Today

Truly the joy of the Lord is our strength. When we are happy, we are more energetic and feel less stressful. When we are happy, we love more, so people enjoy our company. These are just a few benefits of having a joyful spirit.

The only way you can truly maintain a consistently joyful spirit is through Christ Jesus. Sometimes outside circumstances get you pumped up for a little while, but that kind of joy will always fade. The kind of joy these scriptures are talking about will not fade, even when outside circumstances are not so good.

How do you obtain this joy? By being thankful in all things—knowing that God is in control, and trusting Him to do His job. Why do you think children are happy most of the time? If they have good parents, they trust them for everything. I think our heavenly Father is pretty good at parenting, don't you? With trusting comes joy *and all the other benefits!*

From My Journal

March 24, 1997

Today is my birthday. *Thank you, Lord, for giving me life, and blessing me so!* The sun is shining and I have friends and family who love me. We just got back from Nashville, where we finished a new project. My relationship with Rob is solid once again, and I feel close to God. The churches that Dad and Mark pastor are blessed. The bills are paid, and— well, I could go on and on. *Help me to remember my blessings everyday, Lord. Forgive me when I forget.*

What Father Says

"Praise be to the God and Father of our Lord Jesus Christ, who has blessed us in the heavenly realms with every spiritual blessing in Christ" (Ephesians 1:3).

"O Lord, you are my God; I will exalt you and praise your name, for in perfect faithfulness you have done marvelous things, things planned long ago" (Isaiah 25:1).

"The blessing of the Lord brings wealth, and he adds no trouble to it" (Proverbs 10:22).

For You Today

Wow! These scriptures are incredible. *Lord, help us today to believe Your Word and act on it.* Most of us live far short of the blessings of the Lord. One of our problems is that we don't even recognize what they are. We need to pray every day that the Lord will open our spiritual eyes to recognize His blessing.

The devil wants you to concentrate on your troubles instead of your blessings. In doing that, you will walk in defeat instead of victory. *Please Lord; don't let us submit to Satan.* Ungrateful, spoiled children are hard to deal with. By not recognizing and counting our blessings, we become like them. I don't know about you, but it's time for me to grow up. Counting my blessings will be the first step.

From My Journal

March 25, 1997

Yesterday Rob took me to the Sumburger Drive-In for my birthday and had Mary, Deb, and Kathy there to surprise me. We ate dinner together, had birthday cake, and then went to a movie. I'll never forget this birthday. My plan for today is to work out with Kathy and practice my music. I thank God for all His blessings today, and I especially thank Him that He's going to heal my mother of Parkinson's.

What Father Says

"A friend loves at all times, and a brother is born for adversity" (Proverbs 17:17).

"My command is this: Love each other as I have loved you. Greater love has no one than this, that one lay down his life for his friends" (John 15:12–13).

"If one member suffers, all the members suffer with it; or if one member is honored, all the members rejoice with it" (1Corinthians 12:26).

For You Today

As I get older and experience more of life, I am overwhelmed by the value of friendship. Friendship has to be cultivated. You can't expect everyone to come running to you all the time. We need to give the first hello, a pat on the back, a card in the mail, or an invitation to dinner. I don't naturally do these "little things" that make such a difference. I'm working on that weakness in my personality. The Bible tells us that we will reap what we sow. I want to sow good things into people's lives. That should be the goal of every Christian!

Make an effort to do nice things for your friends. Make sure you love and appreciate them, even on their bad days. Extend mercy—you're going to need it in return. I am convinced that it is unhealthy not to have relationships outside your immediate family. We are all brothers and sisters in Christ, and we can learn from each other. Don't you know, the Heavenly Father is pleased when His children are loving each other and having fun together? Remember, sinners are watching us, and the way we relate to each other will help them to want what we have. Be a good friend to a lot of people. We all need friends!

From My Journal

October 5, 1998

God is healing, cleansing, restoring, forgiving, and performing miracles! Over $100,000 was raised from approximately two hundred people for the new worship center at Kingsway Fellowship in Cincinnati. *Praise be to Jesus Christ our Redeemer!* I am making plans to marry Rob Collins on December 1, 1998. Unless God absolutely stops it, I will be Candy Collins. "But one thing I do: forgetting what is behind and straining toward what is ahead, I press on toward the goal to win the prize for which God has called me heavenward in Christ Jesus" (Phil. 3:13–14). I threw out some spiritual garbage today. God used Mary to remind me. *Thank you, Holy Spirit, for speaking wisdom through your children.*

What Father Says

"But your hearts must be fully committed to the Lord our God, to live by His decrees and obey his commands. As at this time" (1 Kings 8:61).

"May the God of hope fill you with all joy and peace as you trust in

Him, so that you may overflow with hope by the power of the Holy Spirit" (Romans 15:13).

For You Today

Just as the people at Kingsway had to trust the Lord for their future finances, I had to trust the Lord for my future. I still do. Again, the wedding didn't take place. With each failed wedding date, I was feeling more like a failure. Sometimes the people we sang to would say hurtful things. This just compounded the feeling of failure. It was through this time that I really had to search the Word about who I am in Christ. I had to cling to scriptures like Romans 15:13 to try and stay hopeful for the future. There were many times I felt hopeless. I had to constantly remind myself that feelings of hopelessness are the devil's lies. Any time you feel like a failure, it's because you are comparing yourself to someone else and not looking at who you are in Christ.

The Bible says in Galatians 6:4, "Each one should test his own actions. Then he can take pride in himself, without comparing himself to somebody else, for each one should carry his own load." The devil knows if he can make us feel like failures, he can keep us living in defeat.

Often we look at other people, their families, their accomplishments, and their finances, compare ourselves to them, and then feel that we have failed. *Do not* do that! Always choose to believe what God's Word says and do it. Remember, the Lord fills us with joy and peace as we trust Him. Our part is to trust Him. Since trusting God is a choice, trust Him and choose to receive peace and joy. Failure and hopelessness will slip away when you do. These feelings have no power over the child of God *if* we choose not to let them!

I have been fasting for about two and a half days. The Lord has shown me that I don't want to commit to things, even things like fasting, for fear of not being able to follow through. *I rebuke and bind that fear in the name of Jesus Christ of Nazareth!* Now that I am into and committed to this fast, I feel very peaceful. It's not easy, and I get hungry, but, oh, the peace! I know the Father is giving me answers through this. I believe that when it's over, I will have received my answers. Mark 11:24 says; "Therefore I tell you, whatever you ask for in prayer, believe that you received it, and it will be yours." Jesus showed me this morning that all my joy and peace are through Him. I had a vision that He took me by my hands and hugged me, and then we held hands facing each other and danced, and laughed and cried. The Lord showed me how everything always points back to Jesus! Even fasting turns to worshipping instead of asking.

What Father Says

"Submit yourselves, then, to God. Resist the devil, and he will flee from you. Come near to God and He will come near to you" (James 4:7–8).

"Come, let us bow down in worship, let us kneel before the Lord our Maker; for He is our God and we are the people of His pasture, the flock under His care" (Psalm 95:6–7).

For You Today

By submitting to God, you resist the devil and he has to flee. The spirit of fear had to take flight in my life as I submitted to God. At that point in my life, God was showing me my fear of commitment because of my fear of making a wrong decision and not being happy. It wasn't about marrying or not marrying; it was about making a commitment either way. Rob and I were in the wilderness of indecision, but I believe that experience served a purpose.

Fear takes different forms, such as fear of the future, fear of finances, and fear of relationships. Once fear strikes, worry and anxiety set in—along with stress. These things come because we fail to submit to God by trusting Him. When we trust God, we don't fear; therefore, fear takes flight.

From My Journal

February 15, 1999

Rob sent me a dozen roses and six white carnations for Valentines Day. We had a long, heartfelt talk over dinner at the *Tumbleweed* restaurant in Chillicothe. Then we went to see the movie *Patch Adams*. It was a beautiful evening. We are dating again, and trusting the Lord to lead us.

What Father Says

"He has made everything beautiful in its time. Also He has put eternity in their hearts, except that no one can find out the work that God does from beginning to end. I know that there is nothing better for them than to rejoice, and to do good in their lives, and also that every man should eat and drink and enjoy the good of all his labor it is the gift of God" (Ecclesiastes 3:11–13).

For You Today

I think it is very important to remember the good times and savor the moments. Rob and I had so much fun together. There were two things I enjoyed most about our relationship. One is that we could discuss the Scriptures together, and the other is that we laughed a lot. I learned so much through those years. I'm thankful for the times we had together. God has put people in your life for "this time" and season. They are a gift from God. Their words are His encouragement. Their acts of kindness were born in His heart. Appreciate your loved ones and friends, and savor the moments.

From My Journal

March 24, 1999

Today is my birthday. I am forty years old, and I can't believe it! Life is what you make it, and, boy, does it go fast! I am in Loydminster, Canada, on a fifteen-day tour, and it is going great. I was just thinking how blessed I am, being surrounded by people who love me. Rob found a grocery store and bought a cake with candles and some toy balloons for my birthday. He is so thoughtful. Mary gave me this journal and a card. Deb sent flowers, which they gave me in the middle of our concert! I am lying in my bunk on the bus, looking at a picture of Jesus smiling at me. What a great day! I'm looking forward to tomorrow.

What Father Says

"My command is this; Love each other as I have loved you. Greater love has no one than this, that one lay down his life for his friends" (John 15:12–13).

For You Today

There isn't any thing more valuable than relationships. Why does this lesson have to be taught over and over? And why are relationships so hard to maintain? Why do we have to work at them constantly—especially with the people closest to us?

God the Father wants a relationship with us more than anything else. He sent His only Son to be crucified for this very reason. That's serious commitment!

We are God's creation, but because of our sin He couldn't have a relationship with us until the blood sacrifice was made. God's desire to have communion with us is beyond our comprehension. We will never really understand the depth of that desire, at least not in this life.

We are made in God's own image; therefore, we have that same longing for close, trusting relationships. We receive that desire from our Father! Satan knows how important relationships are. He knows how much power is available when people are in one accord and how happy and content we are when our relationships are strong and reliable.

Understanding who the true enemy is gives us more patience and understanding. Why are relationships so difficult? First, it is because we have such a desire for them, put there by our Father. The second reason is that Satan's battle plan is to sever the bond we have with other people and with our Father. Satan knows the strength of our relationships with God and with each other spells his demise. Don't let him win!

From My Journal

April 10, 1999

I just had the most wonderful, soothing, satisfying, peaceful, and calming encounter with God through Jesus Christ. While we were talking, I began groaning. This has happened twice in my life. I don't understand my groaning; but according to Romans 8, the Holy Spirit has it under control. I feel so close to Him. *Thank you, Father!*

What Father Says

"In the same way, the Spirit helps us in our weakness. We do not know what we ought to pray, but the Spirit himself intercedes for us with groans that words cannot express. And he who searches our hearts knows the mind of the spirit, because the Spirit intercedes for the saints in accordance with God's will" (Romans 8:26).

For You Today

T he only explanation I have for what happened to me that day is that I was so deep in prayer that the Holy Spirit literally prayed through my voice. As I understand this scripture, it is saying that when we don't know how to pray, the Holy Spirit interprets for us. I think the Lord allows different or supernatural events, such as groaning in prayer or using a prayer language, to strengthen us. After that prayer time, I was totally renewed in spirit, mind, and body. Explaining or analyzing such things is like trying to explain love, heaven, or God himself.

I do not believe these kinds of things have to happen to you as an evidence of the Holy Spirit in your life. I know countless numbers of Spirit-filled Christians who have never experienced any kind of groaning in prayer or speaking in a prayer language. Their loving, kind, selfless lives are complete evidence that God lives in them.

However, don't be caught in the trap of trying to explain away supernatural occurrences that others have had just because you haven't. I once did that, and I realize how wrong I was. Such issues have divided churches and even families. It must grieve the Lord when His people judge each other. What some may need for strengthening, others may not. It's not that complicated, so don't make it an issue. We are all the body of Christ, one family. Let's act like it.

From My Journal

April 22, 1999

I am studying 1 Corinthians, chapters 1–8. I found that it is just as wrong to stuff your body with food as it is to be sexually immoral. These are both sins against the body. In 1 Corinthians 6:12–20, the Word also seems to be plain about the fact that singleness is an easier way of life, allowing more time and concentration to be devoted to God. I never hear preachers addressing this issue. I guess most people get too lonely to accept singleness. I know I get lonely at times.

What Father Says

"I want you to be without care. He who is unmarried cares for the things of the Lord—how he may please the Lord. But he who is married cares about the things of the world—how he may please his wife. There is a difference between a wife and a virgin. The unmarried woman cares about the things of the Lord, that she may be holy both in body and in spirit. But she who is married cares about the things of the world—how she may please *her* husband. And this I say for your own profit, not that

I may put a leash on you, but for what is proper, and that you may serve the Lord without distraction" (1 Corinthians 7: 32–35).

For You Today

This is a tough issue. But God put these scriptures into His Word, so we must deal with them. I was very confused by the New Testament telling us that it is "better not to marry" (1 Corinthians 7:38) while the Old Testament tells us that marriage is ordained by God (Genesis 1:18). I went around this mountain for a long time until one day I asked God to clarify for me why He did that. He seemed to say, "It is because people don't enter into marriage the way it was ordained." It became immediately clear to me. God established the principles of marriage, such as that the husband is to be the spiritual leader of the home and love his wife as Christ loved the church, and that the wife must respect her husband and submit to his spiritual authority.

When marriage partners aren't truly God seekers and do not try to line up with the Word, marriage can be tumultuous. On the other hand, when two people are striving to live according to Bible principles, marriage is the most beautiful relationship there is.

When people are honest, confess, communicate, and seek to walk in agreement with the Word, marriage will be strong. Any other circumstance makes being single an easier way of life, with more time to devote to God. Maybe someday I will have the privilege of entering a godly marriage. Whether that ever happens or not, I will be content—whatever the circumstance (Philippians 4:11). The Holy Spirit empowers us to do so!

From My Journal

May 6, 1999

I am getting ready to have my devotions, and I am expecting revelation. God is so faithful! I am getting rid of a picture that hangs in my living room, entitled "The Little Girl in The Corner." The girl in the picture broke a vase, and looks pitifully like a victim. I bought that picture because it reminded me of myself. It no longer does. I am not a victim. I am free through the blood of Jesus Christ!

What Father Says

"For whatever is born of God overcomes the world. And this is the victory that has overcome the world—our faith" (1 John 5:4).

"In all these things we are more than conquerors through Him who loved us" (Romans 8:37).

For You Today

So many of us live as victims. This mindset goes directly against the Word of God and diminishes the power of the Cross! It is very important for us to search ourselves or, better yet, ask the Lord to search us to find out if we are living with a *victim* mentality. It can be birthed from an attitude of self-pity, which says things like "It's not my fault," "Nobody likes me or wants to be around me," or "Things will never be any different."

If you see yourself as a victim, it is time to repent. God's Word says you are a victor (1 Corinthians 15:57)! Don't choose to diminish the power of the Cross. Do you think Jesus needs to come back and do something more? He does not! We are not victims; according to the Word of God, we are *more* than conquerors. Once we conquer the demons of victimization and self-pity, we'll continue to walk in victory.

When you feel these victim attitudes coming back on you, don't submit to them. Start quoting the scriptures I gave you and *believe* them!

From My Journal

May 15, 1999

Yesterday Mary Jane, her mother Ethel, my aunt Helen, my mother, and I went to Columbus to attend a Joyce Meyer convention. We stayed all day, and it was wonderful! The Spirit of the Lord is so impressive. Joyce is obviously anointed, and I was filled! The day marked an eternal moment in my life. I'm glad my mother was there. I believe mother's healing is complete and that the evidence will be manifested. I am prospering in all areas; and all of this can only be happening through Jesus Christ.

What Father Says

"By humility and the fear of the Lord are riches and honor and life" (Proverbs 22:4).

"But seek first the kingdom of God and His righteousness, and all these things shall be added unto you" (Matthew 6:33).

For You Today

I will not fully understand the subject of healing until I get to heaven. I strongly believe that we are to speak positively and live in hope. God certainly is prospering me in all areas of my life, and my mother is doing great. God is in control.

If we don't live with an attitude of hope and a positive outlook, we become bitter and discouraged—which leads to a life of emptiness and depression.

It is so important that we seek God first. Then, as the Scripture says, everything else will follow. Ask God to help you get to know Him better. The more you know Him, the more you'll want to know Him. And the more you know Him, the less concerned you'll be with issues of healing, prosperity, or anything else. Then the Bible says "all of these things" will follow. Remember, everything lines up behind seeking God!

From My Journal

May 24, 1999

While attending the Joyce Meyer convention in Columbus, Ohio, I felt a powerful rush of the Holy Spirit come over me. I feel so much peace and joy. Certain work and everyday tasks are still hard, but not dreadful. There is always a Comforter. It is exciting! It seems like every scripture I read makes my heart burn within me. I love what the Holy Spirit is doing in me!

What Father Says

"When the Day of Pentecost had fully come, they were all with one accord in one place. And suddenly there came a sound from heaven, as of a rushing mighty wind, and it filled the whole house where they were sitting" (Acts 2:1–2).

For You Today

To try to explain what happened to me that day would be impossible. It is the same Holy Spirit described in Acts chapter 2 who swept through me on May 24, 1999. It seemed that He filled the convention center in Columbus just as He filled the house on the day of Pentecost.

Being filled with the Holy Spirit is so much more than an emotional experience. Although it is very emotional, it is a 24/7 existence. As the days and years have passed, I have enjoyed many powerful moves of the Holy Spirit. These encounters are as fresh and new as the first. I have to continue to live every day in a state of submission to God, search myself, repent, and seek His face. The reward is righteousness, peace, and joy.

Since I have felt the awesomeness of the Holy Spirit's power, I can't settle for anything less. This infilling is available to everyone who is willing to see the truth about themselves, repent, commit themselves wholly to God, and receive what He has promised with an open mind and a tender heart. God is no respecter of persons. He wants all of His children to experience His best!

From My Journal

August 25, 1999

I am reading a book called *The God Chasers* by Tommy Tenny. He talks about the children of Israel remembering how good it was back in Egypt. That was their place of bondage. *Lord, help me to look ahead and leave my places of bondage!*

What Father Says

"Even to this day when Moses is read, a veil covers their hearts. But whenever anyone turns to the Lord, the veil is taken away. Now the Lord is the Spirit, and where the Spirit of the Lord is, there is freedom" (2 Corinthians 3:15–17).

"I will walk about in freedom for I have sought out Your precepts" (Psalm 119:45).

"And the Lord will deliver me from every evil work and preserve me for His heavenly kingdom. To Him be glory forever and ever. Amen!" (2 Timothy 4:18).

For You Today

Why do we stay in bondage of any kind, such as the bondage of fear, the bondage of worry, the bondage of insecurities, the bondage of pride, the bondage of having to be right about everything, the bondage of having to stay young? Why do we have to be in bondage about driving an expensive car, living in a big house, having the prettiest yard, being the best preacher, having the best praise team, or having the biggest church in town? Jesus came to set us free from anything that keeps us bound.

Again, it is our choice. Are we going to believe the devil or believe and walk in the Word of God? Some of the things I have mentioned are not wrong in themselves. It is a matter of whether we control them or whether they control us. Let's make sure to daily give everyone and everything to Jesus. Then we can enjoy the freedom that He came to give us!

From My Journal

December 22, 1999

God gave me a vivid vision of the blood of Christ, washing like a pressurized flow through the strongholds in my life. Praise Him, praise Him, and praise Him! In my mind I could see demons being thrown around, washed away powerless. It is a new day. Look ahead, there's life, joy, peace, fullness, and wholeness, through the blood. *I love you with all my heart, Jesus!*

What Father Says

"In the last days, God says. I will pour out my Spirit on all people. Your sons and daughters will prophesy, your young men will see visions, your old men will dream dreams. Even on my servants, both men and women, I will pour out my Spirit in those days, and they will prophesy" (Acts 2:17–18).

"For though we live in the world, we do not wage war as the world does. The weapons we fight with are not the weapons of the world. On the contrary, they have divine power to demolish strongholds" (2 Corinthians 10:3–4).

For You Today

I woke up this very morning fighting some of the same old battles in my mind that I have fought for years: insecurity, indecision, fear. It lasted about as long as it took me to type that last sentence in my journal entry. You see, the devil doesn't have any new tricks. All he can do is tell the same old lies. It's up to me whether or not I believe him or believe the Word of God!

The Lord is teaching me that my steps are ordered. Writing about this particular journal entry today was not an accident. I remember the day the Lord let me see strongholds being washed out of my life through the blood of Jesus. Through the blood and by submitting to God, I will not be held by Satan, his lies, or negative thinking ever again. That doesn't mean I won't have to fight. The devil will not give up. The Lord is teaching me to recognize the enemy of my soul and how to deal with him.

We have to *think* the Word and *believe* it. But we can't think it if we don't know what it says. That is why it is imperative for the child of God to be a student of His Word. Living and walking in victory is really not that complicated. You just have to know your battle plan. So if you are fighting loneliness, depression, or any other kind of negative thinking, first look up scriptures such as Colossians 1:13, 16–17, 21–23; 2:9–10, 15; and 3:2–4. Speak the Word against the enemy of your soul. It works!

From My Journal

January 26, 2000

I was struggling with a sin I haven't been able to conquer; and my heavenly Father gave me Romans 7:15–25 and Romans 8:1–2. Because of Jesus, my struggle disintegrated and my day was beautiful!

What Father Says

"I do not understand what I do. For what I want to do I do not do, but what I hate I do. And if I do what I do not want to do, I agree that the law is good. As it is, it is no longer I myself who do it, but it is sin living in me. I know that nothing good lives in me, that is, in my sinful nature. For I have the desire to do what is good, but I cannot carry it out. For what I do is not the good I want to do; no, the evil I do not want to do—this I keep on doing. Now if I do what I do not want to do, it is no longer I who do it, but it is sin living in me that does it.

"So I find this law at work: When I want to do good, evil is right there with me. For in my inner being I delight in God's law; but I see another law at work in the members of my body, waging war against the law of my mind and making me a prisoner of the law of sin at work within my members. What a wretched man I am! Who will rescue me from this body of death? Thanks be to God—through Jesus Christ our Lord!" (Romans 7:15–25).

For You Today

If we are honest with ourselves, we will admit that we have had—or now have—some particular sin in our lives that we cannot seem to conquer. We are in good company. As you look at the writings of the Apostle Paul, you'll see that he dealt with the same thing. Although he was struggling in the flesh, he realized with his mind that the blood of Jesus had conquered his fleshly struggles.

He calls the struggle the "law of sin and death." He goes on to say that "the mind controlled by the Spirit is life and peace." See how it works? As a Christian, when you struggle with any kind of sin, you'll probably feel so guilty you won't be able to stand it.

Repent, and realize that your only righteousness is through the blood of Jesus Christ. When you start thinking like that, your mind will be set on what the Spirit desires instead of what your flesh desires. You can conquer sin through Jesus Christ. The guilt will be gone, and you'll have peace.

The battlefield is in the mind. Stay in the Word with humility and repentance. Bring Jesus into your struggles. Confess everything to Him and ask Him to help you. He understands. Though Jesus never sinned, the Bible says that He was tempted with everything that tempts us. He can teach you how to overcome.

From My Journal

March 29, 2000

I turned forty-one five days ago. Through physical eyes, the future appears uncertain; but through spiritual eyes, I see Jesus is already in my future. That is certain and extremely clear. The vision I have of Jesus today is that of a parent reaching for a child who is taking her first steps! *Thank you for reassurance, Father. I delight in you!*

What Father Says

"Consider the blameless, observe the upright; there is a future for the man of peace" (Psalm 37:37).

"Do not let your heart envy sinners, but always be zealous for the fear of the Lord. There is surely a future hope for you, and your hope will not be cut off" (Proverbs 23:17–18).

"For I know the plans I have for you, declares the Lord, plans to prosper you and not to harm you, plans to give you hope and a future" (Jeremiah 29:11).

For You Today

I love these scriptures! Every one of us should commit them to memory. Then, whenever Satan comes against us with insecurity and fear of the future, we can quote these words against him and make him flee. When Satan tempted Jesus in the desert, He fought him off with the Word of God! Is there a better battle plan? Satan will slink away in the face of God's truth. His only power over us is when we believe his lies.

The first scripture talks about being blameless and upright. You might think you aren't even close to that, but the Bible says you are. Colossians 2 tells us that if we have the blood of Jesus applied to our hearts, we are righteous, holy, and above reproach. The Father sees us through Christ's blood. Isn't that a relief? According to Psalm 37:37, there is a future for us. A future of hope and prosperity that will not be cut off. That's God's Word, not mine. People living in Old Testament times had God's promise of a future. But they lived by the law of Moses and had to go through various ceremonies to be declared righteous. You and I live by something even greater: grace. By the shed blood of Jesus on the Cross, and through faith in Him, we are not only adopted into God's family, we are declared righteous—free from the guilt of our past. We have God's covenant promise. We have a hope and a future. God promised it, and He cannot lie (Titus 1:2). His promises are eternal: "Jesus Christ is the same yesterday, today, and forever" (Hebrews 13:8).

Our future is under God's control!

From My Journal

April 11, 2000

I just read through everything I have written in my journal. God has brought me a long way in the past eight or nine years. I want to keep growing and maturing in Jesus Christ. Today the Lord had me watch Marilyn Hickey on TV. She taught on having an excellent attitude. That is exactly what I needed to hear. I know I am going to heaven, but I want my existence on earth to be one of joy, and encouragement to everyone around me! The Lord has been showing me my inconsistencies in this area. *Forgive me, Father.* I can be consistent through Jesus Christ!

What Father Says

"Therefore encourage one another and build each other up, just as in fact you are doing" (1 Thessalonians 5:11).

"When he arrived and saw the evidence of the grace of God, he was glad and encouraged them all to remain true to the Lord with all their hearts" (Acts 11:23).

For You Today

There are so many scriptures about encouragement that I couldn't begin to list them all. I believe many of us fail in this area. Pride and jealousy are the two demonic spirits that keep us from encouraging each other. Ignorance does as well. Many of us do not read the Word enough to understand our duties as children of God. God has set principles in place to help us maintain our joy, and being an encourager is one of them.

When we encourage and edify one another, we not only lift the other person, but we are also blessed. We are affected by the positive words coming out of our own mouths. It constantly amazes me how *everything* God says is for our benefit. Ask the Lord to remove any blinders from your eyes and help you to see the good in the people around you. Encourage and lift them up. Then recognize the joy in your own spirit because of what you are doing. The atmosphere in the home or the work place will be set by the words that are spoken and the attitude that is displayed. A critical spirit is of the devil. Encouragement is of God!

From My Journal

April 28, 2000

This past week the Lord had me repenting over all the discouraging words I have said. It was as if the Holy Spirit was putting the words of repentance right in my mouth. The prayer poured from my spirit. I felt so cleansed. *Continue your correction Father, I long for it!*

What Father Says

"Anxiety in the heart of a man causes depression, but a good word makes it glad" (Proverbs 12:25).

"A soft answer turns away wrath, but a harsh word stirs up anger. The tongue of the wise uses knowledge rightly, but the mouth of fools pours forth foolishness" (Proverbs 15: 1–2).

"A word fitly spoken is like apples of gold in settings of silver" (Proverbs 25:11).

"But I say to you that for every idle word men may speak, they will give account of it in the day of judgment. For by your words you will be justified, and by your words you will be condemned" (Matthew 12:36–37).

For You Today

U nderstanding the power of our words is critical for living a victorious life. According to Proverbs, words can actually affect our state of mind. I don't think this means that the words others say to us can cure depression but that the words we speak have a powerful effect on our well-being. Powerful words from other people can be encouraging—and we all need to speak them to each other. But we must also learn how to speak truth into our own lives. The truth is the Word of God! Know what the Bible says about you. It is difficult to walk around depressed when you realize who you are in Christ. Here are some examples:

I am more than a conqueror—Romans 8:37

I have peace with God—Romans 5:1

I can do all things through Christ—Philippians 4:13

I have all my needs met by God according to His riches in glory in Christ Jesus—Philippians 4:19.

I am being kept strong to the end—1 Corinthians 1:8

If we would speak these kinds of words into our own lives, think what we could do for others!

From My Journal

May 10, 2000

First Corinthians 3:7 says, "Neither he who plants nor he who waters is anything but it is God who gives the increase." The farmer plants, but it is the rain and sun that yields the harvest. You say, "But it still takes the farmer." Who gave life to the farmer? No matter how we look at things, it is always God who gives the increase.

What Father Says

"So the Lord said to him, Who has made man's mouth? Or who makes the mute, the deaf, the seeing, or the blind? Have not I, the Lord?" (Exodus 4:11).

For You Today

According to 1 Corinthians 3:7, God is in control of all things, whether we see those things as good or bad. It is hard to get a grasp on that concept; but when we do, it takes a lot of the pressure off. In any situation we simply trust God. He is in control. It is hard to understand how God could be in control of things such as sickness, death, hunger, or child abuse. He isn't the author of such things, but He is *in control* of them. I believe the reason God doesn't always intervene is because of the power of choice He has given each of us.

It is true that the victims of terrible crimes like rape and child abuse do not have a choice in the matter—but the perpetrator does. As Christians, we have to pray for protection around ourselves and our loved ones. That is a choice also. Often, those who commit terrible acts were victims themselves when they were children. The generational curse keeps getting passed down until someone *chooses* to break that curse of sinful behavior.

I don't understand it all, but I chose to rest in it. It truly is comforting to know that an all-knowing, all-powerful God is in control of things we can't explain.

From My Journal

May 11, 2000

According to 1 Corinthians 4:3, we shouldn't even judge ourselves, let alone other people. I believe it is good to know who we are and why we are the way we are, but over analyzing can get way out of balance. I see where we can become judges of ourselves. But that is God's job. I must stay balanced!

What Father Says

"But with me it is a very small thing that I should be judged by you or by a human court. In fact, I do not even judge myself" (1 Corinthians 4:3).

For You Today

In this verse Paul was writing to the church at Corinth. As I was thinking about this passage, I realized I had a tendency to over analyze myself.

Low self-esteem comes from over-analysis. The opposite extreme is thinking too highly of myself. In my case, low self-esteem was more the issue. Thinking only of myself and my circumstances all the time was very dangerous—it resulted in feelings of depression.

The healthiest thing we can do is seek to know God. And as we learn of Him, we will understand who we are and what our position in life is. I knew that we are not supposed to judge other people, but I never realized the harm that judging myself could lead to. It is our responsibility to keep balance in our lives. Leave the judging to God.

Isn't it great to have a Judge who is forgiving and merciful!

From My Journal

May 16, 2000

Today I asked God why my relationship with my parents was so secure no matter what I did, and my relationship with Him seems to take so much work and discipline. His reply: "There isn't a force working against your relationship with your parents. The enemy doesn't want you to be in close communion with Me; you are too strong when that happens!" Then I asked "Why don't you just keep the enemy at bay?" His answer: "It is not his time to be totally defeated. When that happens it will be heaven."

And that *will* happen!

What Father Says

"But the Lord is faithful, who will establish you and guard you from the evil one" (2 Thessalonians 3:3).

"I will dwell in them and walk among them, I will be their God, and they shall be my people." (2 Corinthians 6:16).

For You Today

I am fortunate to have parents who proved themselves to be there for me no matter what I did or how I acted. It is only because of God that they can be that consistent. Since the devil knows my parents are godly people, he doesn't waste his time fighting my relationship with them. He tries to zero in on my relationship with my heavenly Father through my lack of discipline in the areas of prayer and staying in the Word. If he gets me sidetracked there, everything else in my life will eventually be affected.

Sometimes it is such a struggle for me to read the Bible and pray. That is why I was asking the Lord those questions in my journal. Now I am realizing that God is always there for me—even more than my parents or any other human being.

He gives us the choice as to whether or not we will trust Him and His Word. Satan will always fight us when it comes to prayer and Bible reading because, as the Lord told me that day, we get stronger when we stay in the Word.

There will come a day when Satan will be defeated and we will be in the presence of God forever. To see that day, we need to stay in the Word, believe what we read, and trust God. He is in control whether or not you trust Him. And He loves you, whether or not you know it.

From My Journal

June 28, 2000

I am going through a period in my life where I feel that I don't have any friends outside of my inner circle. I feel left out and sorry for myself. Poor pitiful me! I have never experienced this before. I guess God is breaking that "center of attention" thing in me. Being in the limelight all your life can be damaging. It can be put in perspective only through Jesus Christ! I will take my thoughts captive today (2 Corinthians 10:5). How do I do that? By quoting Scripture and singing songs of praise!

What Father Says

"An unfriendly man pursues selfish ends; he defies all sound judgment" (Proverbs 18:1).

"Let nothing be done through selfish ambition or conceit, but in lowliness of mind let each esteem others better than himself" (Philippians 2:3).

"When we were controlled by the sinful nature, the sinful passions aroused by the law were at work in our bodies, so that we bore fruit for death. But now, by dying to what once bound us, we have been released from the law so that we serve in the new way of the Spirit, and not in the old way of the written code" (Romans 7: 5–6).

For You Today

By submitting to self-pity, I was bearing the fruit of death. The Bible says we have been released from that old way of life so that we can serve in the new way of the Spirit. What is the new way? Righteousness, peace, and joy. The new way is everything that Jesus came to give us. It is our choice. We can think about ourselves all the time, groveling in depression and self-pity, or we can believe the Word and act like the *kings and priests* that we are! My problem that day was thinking about me, me, and me! The limelight that I have been in most of my life is very small compared to some others. But everything is relative.

You may be the center of attention in your home or your workplace. Maybe it's at church or with your circle of friends. By focusing on Jesus, you can make your world revolve around Him—not you. The Bible teaches us to be servants and to put the needs of others before our own. When we learn to act like Jesus by putting others first, we will have more friends than we know what to do with.

Since the time of my journaling, I have made an effort to get to know people outside of my inner circle. The result? My inner circle just keeps getting bigger.

Look to the Word for anything and everything you deal with in life. It's full of answers!

From My Journal

July 9, 2000

The Lord is revealing how beautiful His creation is, and that we are His best creation. As I look in the mirror, I am looking at what He is most proud of and loves the most. As beautiful as the trees, lakes, mountains, animals, beaches and oceans are, in God's eyes I am more beautiful than any of these! As I look at my brothers and sisters in Christ, I see that same beauty. *Lord, help me see past their flesh as you do. Help me to see people as your best creation—a creation that has a will to serve you or not to serve you!*

What Father Says

"So God created man in His own image; in the image of God He created him; male and female He created them" (Genesis 1:27).

For You Today

When self-esteem becomes a problem in your life, read Genesis 1:27. How could we be negative about ourselves when the Bible tells us we are made in the very image of God! The problem is that we measure ourselves by our appearance and outside circumstances such as jobs, successful marriages, finances, and the number of our friends. It is very easy to fall into this trap. Measuring up in all of these areas is impossible. Knowing who we are in Jesus should be the source of our self-esteem.

Do not let our culture dictate your opinion of yourself. You will never be satisfied; you will be depressed. Then Satan will have you where he wants you. The Bible says that through Jesus Christ, you are blessed with every spiritual blessing (Ephesians 1:3); you have peace with God (Romans 5:1); you always triumph in Christ (2 Corinthians 2:14); you can do all things through Christ (Philippians 4:13); you are being kept strong to the end (1 Corinthians1:8); and you are more than a conqueror (Romans 8:37). You are made in the image of God. Go ahead and live like it!

From My Journal

July 18, 2000

The Lord is bombarding me with scriptures about the mind—especially about what to think and say in order to keep it renewed everyday. Today He gave me Colossians 1:13; "He has delivered us from the power of darkness and conveyed us into the kingdom of the Son of His love." The dictionary defines *dark* as: (1) the absence of light—darkness, a dark place, (2) the state of being secret or obscure, often underhand secrecy; also ignorance. We have been delivered from all this through Jesus Christ's death at Calvary. It's real; it happened. I will walk in it!

What Father Says

"He has delivered us from the power of darkness and conveyed us into the kingdom of the Son of His love" (Colossians 1:13).

"For by Him all things were created that are in heaven and that are on earth, visible and invisible, whether thrones or dominions or principalities or powers. All things were created through Him and for Him" (Colossians 1:16).

"For in Him dwells all the fullness of the Godhead bodily; and you are complete in Him, who is the head of all principality and power" (Colossians 2:9–10).

For You Today

Depression is emotional darkness. It is hopelessness and dread. It is a terrible place to be! I have experienced some depression myself. Colossians 1:13 has always been the scripture I cling to when I feel demonic attacks of darkness and depression coming against me. I have already been delivered from the power of darkness! It happened two thousand years ago when Jesus Christ died on the cross. At that moment, I was conveyed into righteousness, peace and joy, in the kingdom of "the Son of His love." Everything He gave me because of my faith in Christ and the Cross is counter to darkness, hopelessness, and dread.

The Bible says that all things were created by God and for God— including principalities and powers. That includes the devil and all his lying demons! Although Satan now opposes God, God has him on a leash. So the only power Satan has over us is what we allow him to have. He is a liar and the Father of lies. The Bible says that we are complete in Jesus Christ and that He is has power over Satan and all of hell.

That power and authority includes the demon of depression! Darkness is the *absence* of light. Jesus *is* the light, and He lives inside you! Believing His Word lets the light of His love shine into your depression or dread.

Jesus, thank you for being the source of our deliverance!

From My Journal

August 1, 2000

The Word of God is so incredible! There is no way a human being could compile such a perfect road map for living! It's not that God has to prove himself, but He certainly did just that. That's how merciful He is. His Word offers proof of His existence. *Thank you Father! I am so impressed!*

What Father Says

"Your Word is a lamp to my feet and a light to my path" (Psalm 119:105).

"So then faith comes by hearing, and hearing by the Word of God" (Romans 10:17).

"How sweet are your words to my taste, sweeter than honey to my mouth!" (Psalm 119:103).

For You Today

A s I get older, I realize more and more that our only guide for truth is the Word of God. After watching the ordeal of the impeachment of a President, I can see how people can make truth anything they want it to be by changing the meaning of words. Can you imagine how chaotic life would be without the inspired and unchanging Word of God? Every lie of the devil would be interpreted as truth in our mind. We would submit to anything our flesh wanted and would completely self-destruct.

Have you ever noticed how miserable people are who live outside of the Bible's boundaries? If you have ever studied the lives of rich and famous people, you know that their stories are usually filled with the same, sad things: addictions, multiple marriages, and broken emotions. People who serve the Lord and live in the truth of God's Word are not exempt from these things; but when they submit to temptation and fall, they know where to turn for deliverance. The Bible has proven itself reliable. The fact that it has stood for thousands of years, through hundreds of translations and languages, and across many cultural lines, is an absolute miracle. God made sure that His Word wouldn't change. It always has been, and always will be, the truth!

From My Journal

September 1, 2000

When I am in a conflict, I realize that it's not the guy in the car next to me that I am fighting against, and it's not the people I work with, live with, or who are members of my family—biological or spiritual. It is not even my circumstances, my finances, or my health that is the real problem. It is principalities, powers, rulers of darkness, and spiritual hosts of wickedness who fight against me and want to rule me. They will not! I stand dressed in the whole armor of God through the blood of Jesus Christ!

What Father Says

"The night is far spent, the day is at hand. Therefore let us cast off the works of darkness, and let us put on the armor of light" (Romans 13:12).

For You Today

How many times have you let the things I listed in my journal entry dictate your actions and reactions? This is something I have to think about, pray about, and deal with practically every day. I guess that is why the Bible tells us not to worry about tomorrow—we have enough to deal with today. The challenges we face are not to ignore the circumstances themselves but to have a right attitude toward them.

For example, I received a notice that my house payment was going to increase. I started crying and threw the notice across the kitchen. At that moment I was submitting to the fear of not being able to make the payment. I was not exercising any faith that God was going to help me. I did not have my armor on, and the fiery darts of Satan were penetrating my mind. I wasn't fighting against the bank or my financial situation, I was fighting against fear. Some people think that seeing *everything* as a spiritual battle is out of balance. Yet I believe that everything *is* spiritual in the sense that God wants to be in all of our circumstances and wants us to trust Him. He said our "steps are ordered by the Lord" (Psalm 37:23).

The next time you find yourself totally frustrated, depressed, or angry, remember who the enemy of your mind, will, and emotions really is; then submit to God by trusting Him. The light of His Word will cause the enemy to flee.

And by the way, I have never missed a house payment!

From My Journal

January 2, 2001

Asking the Father questions and questioning His wisdom and authority are two different things. In Matthew 22 the Pharisees were trying to trap Jesus. It didn't work then, and it won't work now!

What Father Says

"Then the Pharisees went and plotted how they might entangle Him in His talk. And they sent to Him their disciples with the Herodians, saying, 'Teacher, we know that You are true, and teach the way of God in truth; nor do You care about anyone, for You do not regard the person of men. Tell us, therefore, what do You think? Is it lawful to pay taxes to Caesar, or not?" But Jesus perceived their wickedness, and said, 'Why do you test Me, you hypocrites?'" (Matthew 22:15–18).

For You Today

A loving Father will answer His children's questions all day long. Yet if that child throws a fit because he doesn't hear what he wants to hear, the parent will exercise discipline. Sometimes we act like spoiled children when we don't get what we want from God. At other times we try to manipulate God by quoting His own Word to Him along with interpretations of our own making.

We may greedily desire new cars, new homes, and other material things. But God is sovereign. He knows what is best for each one of His children. We can ask Him questions, but we must not question His authority.

The Pharisees were being manipulative in this passage, but Jesus knew exactly what they were doing. When we pray we need to understand that the Father sees the very intent of our hearts. He will not be manipulated. Let's get real and quit acting like spoiled children by questioning God's authority.

From My Journal

January 9, 2001

In Matthew 28: 9–10, I read that the first word out of Jesus' mouth after His resurrection was "Rejoice!" His next words were "Do not be afraid."

What Father Says

"As they went to tell His disciples, behold, Jesus met them, saying, 'Rejoice!' So they came and held Him by the feet and worshiped Him. Then Jesus said to them, 'Do not be afraid. Go and tell My brethren to go to Galilee, and there they will see Me'" (Matthew 28: 9–10).

For You Today

We often wonder what God expects of us even though He has already told us in His Word! When I reviewed my journal and found this entry, I was amazed again at the simplicity of the gospel. The first words from Jesus' mouth were commands to rejoice and to refuse to submit to fear. How simple! The only way we can fulfill these commands is to remain fully baptized in the Holy Spirit. The Bible tells us that He is our Helper. There is no way to rejoice and steer clear of fear without the help of the Holy Spirit. Jesus' bloody death at Calvary made it possible for us to rejoice and not fear. It is our decision to believe.

From My Journal

January 16, 2001

Among the things that I believe the scripture says are these: First, love covers a multitude of sins. (1 Peter 4:8). When we love even the people who have sinned against us, we are the ones who benefit because we have peace. Our love covers their sin against us. The love is stronger than the sin. Second, when Jesus is in our hearts, there is peace. Mark 4:36–40: "When He is in the boat there is peace." No matter what form the storm takes around us—emotions, finances, physical problems, relationship—when He is present there is peace!

What Father Says

"And above all things have fervent love one for another, for 'love will cover a multitude of sins'" (1 Peter 4: 8).

"Now when they had left the multitude, they took Him along in the boat as He was. And other little boats were also with Him. And a great windstorm arose, and the waves beat into the boat, so that it was already filling. But He was in the stern, asleep on a pillow. And they awoke Him and said to Him, 'Teacher, do You not care that we are perishing?' Then He arose and rebuked the wind, and said to the sea, 'Peace, be still!' And the wind ceased and there was a great calm. But He said to them, 'Why are you so fearful? How is it that you have no faith?'" (Mark 4:36–40).

For You Today

"L ove covers a multitude of sins." Those words tell us that our fervent love for each other will keep us out of bitterness and offense. Our love is covering another person's sin against us. We all say and do things we wish we could take back. But if the person you have sinned against loves you fervently, your sin will be covered in their eyes, and that person will continue to walk in peace. You, on the other hand, need to repent.

The anger and confusion that accompanies misunderstanding and broken relationships is like a storm that needs a heavenly calm. For the disciples, the answer was already in their boat: "Now when they had left the multitude, they took Him along in the boat." Peace comes from the presence of the Prince of Peace. Where He is, there is peace.

If Jesus is present in your life, take advantage of that presence by allowing Him to take complete control. Many of us do exactly what the disciples did that day. They spend too much time watching the storm without going to Jesus for help. As soon as we go to Jesus, He will rebuke the storm and we will feel the calm. We do this by getting into the Word, praying, and believing. Our circumstances might not change overnight, but our *view* of those circumstances will!

From My Journal

February 20, 2001

The scripture that jumped out at me today was Luke 11:43. It talks about the Pharisees, who wanted the best seats in the synagogues. Sometimes I want something better for myself than for my brothers and sisters. Sometimes I get envious or discouraged when I don't get the attention or respect I think I deserve. *Forgive me Father for wanting the best seat in the house. In every situation help me think of others. In Jesus name!*

What Father Says

"Woe to you Pharisees! For you love the best seats in the synagogues and greetings in the market places" (Luke 11:43).

For You Today

W e call ourselves *Christians*, and if we truly are Christians we will want to be Christlike in our actions and attitudes. Jesus Christ was all about loving, serving, and putting others first. So often the Lord has to remind me that I am being more Pharisaical than Christlike.

The Pharisees cared only about themselves, their titles, and the respect of the people. Doesn't that sound a lot like the church today? We need to daily search ourselves and make sure that we are being like Christ.

Putting others first is not that difficult. It takes such forms as respecting the opinions of others; including them in our prayer; watching for ways that we can be of help to them; giving financially to help relieve their financial struggles; or giving of our time to relieve their burdens.

As you read the Scriptures, look for ways that Christ met the needs of others—and then follow His example.

From My Journal

March 19, 2001

The Lord revealed to me today that when people lash out at me, I am not the victim. The person attacking is the victim. That person may be the victim of insecurity or bondage. I must have compassion on them!

What Father Says

"Then Jesus said, 'Father forgive them for they do not know what they do'" (Luke 23: 34).

For You Today

When I feel under attack, it takes every bit of the Holy Spirit in me to think straight and to stay in control. There are times when each of us needs a rebuke, but as my brother John said, "If it's not done in love, it's an attack—even if it is the truth."

If we have trouble receiving even a truthful rebuke, how can we possibly deal with undeserved attacks without the help of the Holy Spirit? When someone lashes out at you and you have done nothing to deserve a rebuke, try to remember that the person is speaking through frustration. There is jealousy or insecurity of some kind that is triggering their behavior. It is difficult, but if we can look at them through Jesus' eyes at that moment, we can have forgiveness and compassion for them—even during the attack.

Jesus did that. The sinless Savior didn't deserve one mocking word. He didn't deserve the nails. He didn't deserve the thorns. He looked beyond the abuse to have compassion on the abuser. As a Christian, you can do the very same thing when you are under attack. The power of the Holy Spirit within you makes it possible.

From My Journal

May 18, 2001

Today I came face to face with my fear of the future. I have renounced that fear through the authority of Jesus Christ. I have no fear of marriage, and I have no fear of singleness. I am in Jesus, and He is in me!

What Father Says

"I have been crucified with Christ; it is no longer I who live, but Christ lives in me; and the life which I now live in the flesh I live by faith in the Son of God, who loved me and gave Himself for me" (Galatians 2:20).

"There is no fear in love; but perfect love casts out fear, because fear involves torment. But he who fears has not been made perfect in love" (1 John 4:18).

For You Today

A s I mentioned in the introduction to this book, I was delivered from fear. By this point in my life, I was able to recognize fear and fight against it with spiritual weapons. Through the authority of Jesus Christ, we have power to renounce such things as fear in our lives.

You may be facing fear related to something like finances, your marriage, your job, or your health. Whatever it is, recognize the enemy behind the fear and face him head on through the blood of Jesus Christ. Fear becomes a stronghold in our lives—a deception in our root belief system that serves as a base of operations for Satan's attack (see 2 Corinthians 10:3–5). Believe the Word, not Satan's lies!

From My Journal

July 15, 2001

The Lord showed me that I am in the bondage of indecision. Rob and I keep remaining in or going back into that bondage to indecision every time we cancel a wedding date—or fail to set one. Joyce Meyer says: "We need to press through the wilderness to the Promised Land." For us, that will mean making a decision and not going back!

What Father Says

"For the Lord our God is He who brought us and our fathers up out of the land of Egypt, from the house of bondage, who did those great signs in our sight, and preserved us in all the way that we went and among all the people through whom we passed" (Joshua 24:17).

"Have I not commanded you? Be strong and of good courage; do not be afraid, nor be dismayed, for the Lord your God is with you wherever you go" (Joshua 1:9).

For You Today

There is nothing worse in this life than living in bondage. Mine was indecision. Living in bondage is the complete opposite of living in faith and freedom. The Bible tells me that the yoke of Christ is easy and the burden is light. It also tells me that I have complete freedom in Jesus Christ. I was so fearful and confused about whether to be married or to remain single. As I look back, I realize that, although the decision was painful to make, once it was done made, the fear and bondage disappeared immediately.

Make sure your decisions in life line up with the Word. Pray, *decide*, and then trust God for the outcome!

From My Journal

July 24, 2001

Yesterday was supposed to be my wedding day. The plans were made, and John's wife, Glenda, my nieces Sheri and Mandy, Julia, Mom, Kim, Marlene, and my hairdresser, Lyn, had John and Glenda's house beautifully decorated. The people were gathered, and the food was prepared. Yet that very afternoon, it was apparent that I had no peace. I can't speak for Rob, but the hardest decision I have ever made in my life was to call it quits!

We probably couldn't have gotten through the day without my brother Mark and his wife, Nicki. They both have so much God-led wisdom. At 7:30 p.m. we made the announcement that we didn't feel right about doing this. Our parents were so supportive, and the people followed suit. Rob and I had been a couple for the past ten years. I gave my diamond back, but my heart hasn't quite fallen in line. I feel pain and tenderness today, but I also feel peace. We have finally made it out of the wilderness of indecision.

What Father Says

"I cried to the Lord with my voice, and He heard me from His holy hill. I lay down and slept; I awoke for the Lord sustained me" (Psalm 3:4–5).

"The Lord is near those who have a broken heart, and saves such as have a contrite spirit" (Psalm 34:18).

"Have I not commanded you? Be strong and of good courage; do not be afraid, nor be dismayed, for the Lord your God is with you wherever you go" (Psalm 1:9).

For You Today

If you are going through the kind of emotional pain that I described in my journal, you must cling to the Scripture. Memorize it, get it in your soul (your mind, your will, and your emotions) and believe it. There is no way I could have made it through that time without the Holy Spirit and the Word of God. I would have plummeted into deep depression, *but I didn't!* More challenges lay ahead, but I know that if I can make it through the emotional pain of calling off a marriage, you can make it through your situation!

Think about the most painful decision that you have ever made—or will make. How would absolute confidence in God and His Word and His direction to your inner spirit change the situation? If you have already made that painful decision, trust God for the healing of your negative reactions. If you have yet to make that decision, let God's Word direct you. Follow His inner voice—which is peaceful and assuring, not troubling.

From My Journal

July 25, 2001

I went to Bible study last night and told the group that I felt the need to give Rob some space for healing and so I wouldn't continue attending. With Rob attending the same church, it would be awkward. The *aloneness* struck after that. I still feel peace deep inside that I made the right decision. Abba Father will fill the void. It is exciting to think of what He is going to do!

What Father Says

"You keep him in perfect peace, whose mind is stayed on You, because he trusts in you. Trust the Lord forever, for the Lord, the Lord is everlasting strength" (Isaiah 26:3–4).

For You Today

Christians can maintain peace no matter what their circumstances. Having the Holy Spirit living inside us is such an awesome thing! We very seldom tap into the power made available to us through Jesus Christ. I loved that Bible study group. It was something Rob had started in Washington Court House, and I felt very much a part of it. When you travel a lot, having that kind of a fellowship is important. It was the first time I had ever felt so much a part of something outside our ministry. It was devastating to tell them I didn't feel that I should come back.

In my aloneness, I could only cling to the hope that the Father was working on my behalf. I was constantly in the Word, listening to preaching tapes and worship music. It works! God sustained me through that time and gave me another Bible study group with whom to be involved.

We all go through difficult times in life, but as Christians we can be assured that God is working on our behalf. Keep your mind focused on Him and He will keep you in perfect peace.

From My Journal

July 31, 2001

God is so good to me. He speaks through my brothers and sisters on my behalf. Mary's niece, Renee Loyd, sent me a card and scripture that made it seem as if she knew exactly where I was and what I was thinking. The scripture was Isaiah 10:3. The application to this scripture in her study Bible reads like this: "Rejoice because you have peace with God! Celebrate God's forgiveness for you. Demonstrate God's peace to others through your relationships. Help your coworkers and family to meet their needs. Relieve the disappointments of others!" The Lord awakened Renee at 4:00 a.m. with this message for me.

Thank you, Father, for loving me so much.

What Father Says

"And the ransomed of the Lord shall return and come to Zion with singing, with everlasting joy on their heads. They shall obtain joy and gladness, and sorrow and sighing shall flee away" (Isaiah 35:10).

For You Today

What a promise! If we would simply believe what the Word says about us, we would get through the tough times so much quicker. We all go through rough spots, but Jesus said His yoke is easy and His burden is light. The valleys in my life have given me proof that I can trust God and that He cares. My part is to turn to Him!

Too many times we let ourselves sink into despair instead of becoming proactive and getting into the Word—and, even more important, letting the Word get into us! Sorrow and sighing did "flee away" because I am one of the ransomed of the Lord.

And so are you!

From My Journal

August 6, 2001

Mary Jane, John, and I were flying from Colorado to Dallas when Mary and I found ourselves seated next to a lady pastor named Phyllis. Mary's seat was supposed to have been John's, but he insisted that she take it. What a God thing! During the entire flight, Pastor Phyllis ministered to Mary and me. She encouraged us to keep doing what we are doing no matter what the circumstances, and to always sing as unto the Lord. I thought about her all day yesterday. God honored our concerts spiritually and financially. To Him be the glory! He also helped us make it through a grueling schedule with no hitches. Our Father is so good.

What Father Says

"Therefore comfort each other and edify one another, just as you also are doing" (1 Thessalonians 5:11).

"Therefore if there is any consolation in Christ, if any comfort of love, if any fellowship of the Spirit, if any affection and mercy, fulfill my joy by being likeminded, having the same love, being of one accord, of one mind" (Philippians 2:1–2).

For You Today

When you are going through a painful time—as I was at that point in my life—and you seek God daily for comfort, sit back and watch how many people He will send your way. God speaks not only through His Word but also through His obedient children. I have been on the receiving end, and I want to make sure my spiritual antenna is up so I can also be on the giving end. If you are hurting, stay in the Word and be open to your brothers and sisters in Christ. Also, as you are comforted and edified, make sure you are available and obedient in doing the same for someone who needs *you*.

From My Journal

August 8, 2001

I have had to do a lot of spiritual warfare this morning. God is so good. He doesn't think thoughts of evil confusion for me but of a future and a hope (Jeremiah 29:11). My mother called this morning with this verse: "Happy is he who has the God of Jacob for his help, whose hope is in the Lord his God" (Psalm 146:5). *Thank you, Lord, for telling my mother to call me.* Thank you, Mother, for being obedient!

What Father Says

"Have I not commanded you? Be strong and of good courage; do not be afraid, nor be dismayed, for the Lord your God is with you wherever you go" (Joshua 1:9).

For You Today

The Word of God tells us in 2 Corinthians 10:3–5, "For though we walk in the flesh, we do not war according to the flesh. For the weapons of our warfare are not carnal but mighty in God for pulling down strongholds, casting down arguments and every high thing that exalts itself against the knowledge of God, bringing every thought into captivity to the obedience of Christ." Spiritual warfare takes place in our minds. At the time of this journal entry, I was fighting loneliness. I had to stay in the Word constantly. It is my sword, my spiritual weapon against the lies of the devil.

When he comes against you with negative thoughts about yourself, find scriptures such as I have given you today and quote them out loud. Satan is out to destroy our self-image. I believe that is his chief strategy against us. He is a liar! Believe what the Word of God says about you. It's the truth!

From My Journal

August 13, 2001

I went to bed last night with heaviness in my heart, and I woke up the same way. But then I received a card in the mail from my brother Mark's Secretary, Amber. And I opened Joyce Meyer's monthly newsletter, which says: "Don't let the devil steal your faith and keep you from enjoying your life." The scriptures from the letter were Isaiah 41:10 and Psalm 121: 7–8. My Father loves me so much, and He is always looking out for me!

What Father Says

"Fear not, for I am with you; Be not dismayed, for I am your God. I will strengthen you, yes, I will help you, I will uphold you with My righteous right hand" (Isaiah 41:10).

"The Lord shall preserve you from all evil; He shall preserve your soul. The Lord shall preserve your going out and your coming in from this time forth, and even forevermore" (Psalm 121: 7–8).

For You Today

God is always speaking to us, but too often we do not take the time to listen. The Lord knew I had gone to bed with emotional heaviness and had awakened the same way. So what did He do? He spoke to me through a card from a friend and a newsletter in the mail. Nothing could be plainer: He spoke peace to me through the words of another.

God speaks through His Word and through the obedience of His children. He will also speak to us through a still, small voice—the gentle whisper of the Holy Spirit. Any good and positive thought that goes through your mind is from God. Listen to it and speak it out if there is opportunity to do so.

The scriptures I have given are for *you*! Receive them, believe them, and live as if your life depended on them.

From My Journal

August 30, 2001

The last fifteen days have been eventful, to say the least. Rob, my former fiancé, quit the group, and last weekend was our first trip without him. It is very difficult, and I miss him deep inside. Chad Walters came with us for the first time. He is such a sweet person and has a lot of potential. God is doing something, and I hope he reveals it to us quickly. I pray He will help me walk in confidence with the decisions I have made. He will!

We have to put a twenty-thousand-dollar transmission in our bus. I asked the Lord this morning to supply the money. I am looking forward to the weekend because we will be blessed, we will be anointed, and things will be revealed. God will speak, we will listen, and finances will be provided! Our Father is always faithful! *I love you, Jesus the Christ. You are my Lord and Savior.*

What Father Says

Psalm 23

The Lord is my Shepherd; I shall not want. He makes me to lie down in green pastures; He leads me beside the still waters. He restores my soul; He leads me in the paths of righteousness for His name's sake. Yea, though I walk through the valley of the shadow of death, I will fear no evil; For You are with me; Your rod and staff, they comfort me. You prepare a table before me in the presence of my enemies; You anoint my head with oil; My cup runs over. Surely goodness and mercy shall follow me all the days of my life; And I will dwell in the house of the Lord forever.

For You Today

A positive confession is imperative for the Christian's life and faith. The 23rd Psalm is evidence of just how vital it is. At the time I wrote this journal entry, I was in a lot of emotional pain. Despair and loneliness were constantly looming, and it took everything in me to keep fighting. A *positive confession* was one of my weapons. As you can see, my journal entry began with doubt and worry but ended with faith in what God was about to do.

Begin making positive confession by monitoring your conversation throughout the day. Notice whether you are speaking blessing into your life or words full of negativism. Do you speak blessings into the lives of others? There is already enough negativism in our world. Speak positive words for a *change*.

From My Journal

October 30, 2001

Yesterday I asked the Lord for more power. He said, "Your power will increase as your love increases." It is so obvious why the Lord spoke to me about love. *Father God, in the name of Jesus Christ, help me to get my armor in place. I am fighting anger. Anger turns to bitterness and I will not go there, with your help Holy Spirit. Father, you love me so much. Keep me out of self-pity, I pray.*

What Father Says

"And we have known and believed the love that God has for us. God is love, and he who abides in love abides in God, and God in him" (1 John 4:16).

For You Today

Going through the agony of a wedding day breakup was unbelievably painful. My emotions revolved from sadness to anger to loneliness to self-pity and back again. The Word was my only comfort. When we go through emotionally painful times, I believe the devil sends every available demon in hell to destroy us. When we are wounded, Satan knows it. His purpose is to strike the final blow. But here's the truth: "Greater is He that is in me than he that is in the world." That is the Word of God, and you can count on it!

Anger, bitterness and self-pity are dangerous emotions that can take over our lives and become our identities. We have to get into the Word of God and fight these spirits with a passion. The Word is your sword; use it to strengthen your faith, maintain peace, believe truth, be assured of your salvation, and know the will of God. There is no way Satan can defeat us when we have our Sword in hand. And we have the Holy Spirit to give us power for the battle. Draw from Him!

From My Journal

December 26, 2001

This is my first Christmas in ten years without Rob. The Holy Spirit spoke to me and said, "Celebrate the birth of your Savior. Do not make Him feel sad by being depressed and lonely on His birthday—He came to abolish all such things." I chose to listen and to be obedient. It was a beautiful Christmas. *Jesus, I hope you enjoyed it as much as I did!*

What Father Says

"'No weapon formed against you shall prosper, and every tongue which rises against you in judgment you shall condemn. This is the heritage of the servants of the Lord, and their righteousness is from Me' says the Lord" (Isaiah 54:17).

For You Today

You may wonder why I chose this particular scripture when the subject is loneliness. Loneliness is one of the weapons Satan uses against us. When we read scriptures like this and realize that God has our back, Satan's weapon can't succeed and we defeat loneliness.

All of us go through times when we feel alone. When we do, it is imperative that we get into the Word of God and believe what it says. Through faith in Christ, you are never alone—Jesus is always with you. How do I know? Because He said so: "I will never leave you or forsake you" (Hebrews 13:5). Jesus was forsaken by His own father on the Cross so that He could identify with you in your times of loneliness. Believe His Word when Satan attacks you with loneliness.

Do not let loneliness turn into self-pity and then into depression. Recognize your enemy as soon as he comes against you. Your strategy is faith in the Word!

From My Journal

December 29, 2001

Today I was feeling loneliness again, and I confessed it to the Father. The Lord had me read in John 4 about the woman at the well. Jesus told her He had water she could drink of and never thirst again. We think a husband, family, or certain relationships will remove our loneliness, but in reality only Jesus can do that. The loneliness can return, no matter what your situation. But Jesus will quench that loneliness. It's a good thing I have Jesus. The Lord also said to me, "Do not draw from the wrong well."

What Father Says

"Jesus answered and said to her, 'Whoever drinks of this water will thirst again, but whoever drinks of the water that I shall give him will never thirst. But the water that I shall give him will become in him a fountain of water springing up into everlasting life'" (John 4:13–14).

For You Today

The Pfeifers take a break of about two weeks during the Christmas holidays. I live alone, so once the parties were over, I had a lot of spare time on my hands. Because my broken wedding day was still a fresh memory, staying on top of loneliness and my feelings of insecurity about ever having that "special someone" was an everyday battle. As the Father told me, I had been drawing from the wrong well.

We will never find long-term security in any relationship outside of Jesus Christ. God was faithful to me through that time, but I had to seek Him. I couldn't just lay around feeling sorry for myself and expect Him to rain down revelation. I had to get up every morning, read my Bible, and talk to God as if He were sitting in the room with me.

If you are going to draw from the well of living water, you'll need absolute faith that He is with you and hears you when you pray. The loneliness left me that day after I had fellowship with my Father. I drank from the right well!

From My Journal

January 26, 2002

I am having some rough days, but none without victory! I have to stay in prayer and in the Word. I have to keep my spiritual armor in place and do spiritual warfare. Today, through the authority of Jesus Christ, I fought off the evil spirit of loneliness and the fear of loneliness. They cannot stay where Jesus is. *I couldn't make it without you, Jesus, and I will never have to.*

What Father Says

"And He said to me, 'My grace is sufficient for you, for My strength is made perfect in weakness.' Therefore most gladly I will rather boast in my infirmities, that the power of Christ may rest upon me. Therefore I take pleasure in infirmities, in reproaches, in needs, in persecutions, in distresses, for Christ's sake. For when I am weak, then I am strong" (2 Corinthians 9–10).

For You Today

During those days after the breakup, I was fighting loneliness day by day and sometimes even hour by hour. The key is I was *fighting*. I refused to give up when Satan attacked me. Was I weakened by the attacks? Sure. Emotionally and physically, I was worn down by the constant doubts the devil thrust upon me. But just like the Apostle Paul, my weaknesses became a source of strength. The power of Christ was resting upon me. I realized that Jesus was in this battle with me. I really wasn't alone. I could trust Him, and He would never fail me.

The Word says, "above all, take the shield of faith." The reason I made it through that season of my life was because of my faith in God and His Word. It is true; the Word is our weapon to keep fear and loneliness at bay. When the Word talks about renewing your mind, it means changing your mind to focus on Christ until He either changes you or changes your situation. Stay in the Word, and believe it. Soon you'll be strong!

From My Journal

February 27, 2002

When the seasons of our lives change, the adjustments can take a long time. It seems that trusting God for my companion is the adjustment I am making at this time. The challenge I face is learning to bounce things off of Jesus instead of another person. Learning to curl up at night knowing He is there, waking up in the morning and speaking my first words to Him. The reality of it is I can live a peaceful, joyous life without another person—but not without Jesus!

What Father Says

"For we do not have a High Priest who cannot sympathize with our weaknesses, but was in all points tempted as we are, yet without sin. Let us therefore come boldly to the throne of grace, that we may obtain mercy and find grace to help in time of need" (Hebrews 4:15–16).

For You Today

Have you ever said, "But you just don't know how I feel!" Sometimes even our closest friends don't really understand us. They have one perspective, and we have another. But there is a friend who *does* know how we feel: Jesus. When I think about His life, I can't imagine how lonely He must have felt. There wasn't any room in the inn for Him, so He was born in a manger. Sometimes the people closest to him, His disciples, didn't understand who He was and what He was doing. His own brother, James, didn't believe in Him at the first. Jesus prayed alone in the Garden of Gethsemane and poured out His heart to his Father. Our Lord was nailed to a cross— alone—because His followers all abandoned him.

We must realize who we are in Christ Jesus so that we don't try to draw our identity from our relationships with other people or from anything else. As long as we gain self-esteem from our position in life, we will not be secure. We'll be fighting a battle we cannot win!

I can be either single or married and still be whole. I can drive a new car, a used car, or no car at all and still be whole. I can live in a small house or a mansion, be a white-collar employee or a blue-collar employee and still be whole. Every emotional need we have can be satisfied by the Father. Go boldly to His throne. Tell Him how you feel, and tell Him what you need.

From My Journal

March 25, 2002

Yesterday was my birthday. I turned forty-three years old, and I had a *wonderful* day. But after I got home, I ate, picked up my mail, sat down at the kitchen counter, and began to weep. I have been dreading coming home to an empty house. I opened a card from Delilah Sheridan that said, "God blesses him with strong support whose love for Christ is undimmed. Remain focused as you seek the Lord." *Thank you, Father, for obedient children like Delilah Sheridan.*

What Father Says

"'Behold, I stand at the door and knock. If anyone hears My voice and opens the door, I will come in to him and dine with him, and he with Me. To him who overcomes I will grant to sit with Me on My throne, as I also overcame and sat down with My Father on His throne'" (Revelation 3:20–21).

For You Today

Delilah Sheridan is the mother of Stan Sheridan, who traveled with us for about seven years. She lives in Alabama, and I live in Ohio, so we never have much contact. Because of our connection with Stan, she had heard about my wedding not working out. Her card arrived *six months* after all that happened. I am amazed at how God constantly watches out for us. He knew I would walk into that empty house and be affected by it that very evening. He laid it on Delilah's heart to send me a card, which arrived right on time. Delilah heard the voice of the Lord and was obedient. It is important for us to be mindful of the little things. I was able to overcome at that moment because of Delilah's obedience. Let's make it a goal to be a blessing to other people—every day.

From My Journal

March 27, 2002

There is something about the sound of building that I really like. My neighbors are building a new home next door to me. Each morning I hear hammers, saws, and big equipment being used. It is exciting; it is the sound of hope, an expectation of things to come. It is as if the Lord is saying to me right now, "This is where you are. I am building things in your life. Do not be discouraged; be encouraged when you are under construction." If you have ever built a home, you know things can go wrong and deadlines sometimes are not met, but through all the headaches there remains an excitement and expectation of things to come. *Jesus, please empower me to walk in that today!*

What Father Says

"Being confident of this very thing, that He who has begun a good work in you will complete it until the day of Jesus Christ" (Philippians 1:6).

For You Today

I f you have been discouraged lately about who you are and how you act and react to situations, or if you think people don't like you and in general feel like a failure, remember that if you are a child of God, He is always working on you!

Be excited about what God is doing in your life instead of being discouraged. Believe the Bible; it is the truth. Believing the promises of the Bible is like taking emotional medication, medication like none you will find in a pharmacy!

And the great thing is, God will never give up on you. If you'll let Him, He'll keep working on you "until the day of Jesus Christ." Victory day! And don't be discouraged about the progress of the construction. God completes His projects in His own time—and that is always the right time!

From My Journal

April 15, 2002

I guess I could refer to this day as a "Blue Monday," but I won't. One of my very dearest friends in the world (and my hairdresser), Lyn Brackens, came to tell me that Rob is engaged to be married in August. This was a very difficult thing for her to do because she hates to see me hurting. But she didn't want me to hear it from just anybody. It was a very brave thing for her to do, and I am thankful to have friends like her.

Everyone in this small town already knows. We just came in off the road and I received a card in the mail from my sister-in-law, Glenda. It couldn't have come at a better time, as she assured me that she and John would always be there for me. I believe her! It amazes me how our Father orchestrates our lives right down to a visit from a friend to a card in the mail. *Powerfully spoken words that nourish and heal are what I thank you for, Jesus.* I have been a needy person at certain times in my life, but now I need Jesus. All my dependency is on Him. He will supply all of my needs. That is what the Word says. And if I believe Glenda, why wouldn't I believe God! I wish Rob the best, and I thank him for the good times we shared.

What Father Says

"I have set the LORD always before me; Because He is at my right hand I shall not be moved. Therefore my heart is glad, and my glory rejoices; My flesh also will rest in hope. For You will not leave my soul in Sheol, Nor will You allow Your Holy One to see corruption. You will show me the path of life; In Your presence is fullness of joy; At Your right hand are pleasures forevermore" (Psalm 16:8–11).

For You Today

On that "Blue Monday," I got both disturbing news and encouraging news on the same day. That happens often in our lives. God follows up some discouragement with encouragement. He knows how much we can bear. He knows how weak we really are. He made us, so He knows how to take care of us.

If we can take our thoughts captive and believe this truth, our hearts will be filled with joy, our mouths will sing praises, and we will live in peace.

From My Journal

April 26, 2002

Ｇod is teaching me through everyday tasks that I can do all things through Christ who gives me strength. I am amazed at what the Father is helping me accomplish around the house. It is exciting! It is such a beautiful day, and there is not a cloud in the sky. My French doors are open, and my neighbor Glenn's horses are grazing in the field behind my house. Everything is already green, and the birds are singing. *Father, thank you for Your beautiful creation!*

What Father Says

"Every good and perfect gift is from above, and comes down from the Father of lights, with whom there is no variation or shadow of turning. Of His own will He brought us forth by the word of truth, that we might be a kind of first fruits of His creatures" (James 1: 17–18).

For You Today

I am so in awe of God's creation. That you and I are His greatest creation is beyond my understanding. When I look at the ocean in the Bahamas, the mountains of the western United States, or the redwood trees in the Sequoia National forest, I feel insignificant compared to their massive beauty.

When I stand in the middle of God's creation, I focus on what is around me, not on the problems of the day—or my insecurities. As a matter of fact, I feel extremely secure when I think about serving a Creator that never changes. Change isn't easy for us. It makes us feel insecure and restless. I've felt that way. And I have taken spiritual authority over those thoughts by trusting God's power over them. God's Word doesn't change either. Every verse is as true today as it was in the beginning. I'm excited about living in a world like this with promises like His!

From My Journal

August 15, 2002

We are in camp meeting at my brother Mark's church, and last night he ordained my former fiancé Rob and his wife to be. It was the first time I had seen her, making it extremely awkward and difficult. I still love him.

I woke up this morning feeling low and lonely. I have learned what my first line of defense is: prayer and the Word. I told the Lord exactly what was on my mind and how I was feeling. I felt impressed to get out a women's devotional Bible that I don't normally read. I have a New King James Version that I usually read and study from. When I opened my devotional Bible, I noticed that our office manager, Julia Dawson, had given it to me for Christmas in 1997. Right below that information was the scripture reference Isaiah 58:11. I quickly turned to Isaiah 58, read through the chapter, and ran to get my journal because God was giving me so much revelation.

I opened my journal and looked at the bottom of the page where a scripture reference had been randomly printed. I couldn't believe my eyes—it was Isaiah 58:11! I had a shoutin' spell, as they used to say when I was a kid. When I was praying this morning, I asked God if my life counted for anything, especially if I should live and die without having children to leave behind. I also addressed Him about feeling so alone physically. This is what

Isaiah 58:11 says: "The LORD will guide you always; He will satisfy your needs in a sun scorched land and will strengthen your frame. You will be like a well watered garden, like a spring whose waters never fail." That is the truth! That is what God is saying to me, and I believe the Word, not the devil! In 1997, He was preparing me for this day in 2002. He laid it on Julia's heart to get me this particular Bible. God knew all along that this day would come, and He had it all under control. A well watered garden bears much fruit and feeds a lot of people.

What Father Says

"The Lord will guide you continually, and satisfy your soul in drought, and strengthen your bones; You shall be like a watered garden, and like a spring of water, whose waters do not fail" (Isaiah 58:11).

For You Today

I won't add much to this journal entry, other than to say that the Word of God is for everyone who will read it and believe it. When we get desperate enough, we will hear what the Lord is trying to say to us. He is always speaking, but we are not always listening. God's Word is life, and He will speak life into us everyday if we will seek Him. Be a "well watered garden." The result will be a fruitful life that will bless everyone around you!

God knows exactly what you need; and He knows exactly when you need it.

From My Journal

December 31, 2002

As we head into the New Year, I have a strong desire to pray in the Father's will. I want my desires to line up with His will. And I have learned not to have preconceived ideas about what that is!

What Father Says

"For I know the thoughts that I think towards you, says the Lord, thoughts of peace and not of evil, to give you a future and a hope" (Jeremiah 29:11).

For You Today

The title of this devotional book is *Getting It Right*. God has just the right word for me. Now I must learn to get it right—to trust God when He says He has thoughts of peace and not of evil, thoughts of giving me a future and a hope. If you want to get it right, trust the Lord, believe His Word, repent when you mess up, and seek Him with all your heart.

You'll get it right!

Epilogue

Many months have past since I began writing this devotional book. As I review my first journal entry from 1992, it is hard for me to believe how many years have gone by and how much my views have changed. God keeps working on me, and as I am open to His teaching. Our bodies get weak and deteriorate, but as we submit to God, our spirits grow stronger and stronger. Life just gets better!

My life is very full and rich these days. I walk in victory, and the Father continues to gently correct me. We are eternal beings and this life is only the conception. As Joyce Meyer says, "We are in training for reigning."

Contact Information

Candy Pfeifer

The Pfeifers
120 West Court Street
Washington C.H., Ohio 43160
Phone: (740) 335-9641
Fax: (740) 335-2024
E-mail: email@pfeifers.com
Website: http://www.pfeifers.com